Theologian, historian, and ecumenist, Rev. George H. Tavard, A.A., is Professor of Theology at Methodist Theological School in Ohio. He is a member of many professional associations, including the American Theological Society and the American Catholic Historical Society. He was an Expert at the Second Vatican Council, and is the author of seventeen books and 72 articles which have been published in the United States and Europe.

A Way of Love

A WAY OF LOVE

George H. Tavard

ORBIS  BOOKS

Maryknoll, New York

Copyright © 1977, Orbis Books, Maryknoll, N.Y. 10545
All rights reserved
Manufactured in the United States of America

Library of Congress Cataloging in Publication Data

Tavard, George Henri, 1922–
   A way of love.

   Bibliography: p.
   1. Love (Theology)   I. Title.
BV4639.T29   241'.6'77   76-22542
ISBN 0-88344-700-2

To

Eileen Tyrrell Scheib

Contents

Preface

Several periods in the history of Christian thought have been marked by an abundance of writings on the nature of love. We are in such an era. Psychological, psychoanalytical, sociological, philosophical, phenomenological, literary, theological, and biblical studies on love have been published during the last few decades. The hidden causes of such an interest in love would themselves deserve serious investigation. Do we intellectualize love because we do not experience it? Do we seek shelter from the deprivation of love among books by the mass media, which tend to reduce love to sex and sex to pornography? Or is an authentic rediscovery of love taking place, heralding the end of what Pitrim Sorokin called the "sensate" culture, that is, a culture characterized by the general decadence of sensitivity? Is Christian theology on the verge of formulating a new version of the Gospel of Love that has been identified with the popular image of Jesus? Is Christian moral thinking about to promote a more refined conception of obedience and law, in which St. Augustine's suggestion, "Love and do what you will," will finally become practicable? Are Christians discovering the importance of love among other religions, thus slowly entering an age of wider ecumenical concerns and possibilities? Are Christian

faith and the works of love inspired by it ready to sup-
plant the Marxist philosophy of history as the basic motive for liberation from injustice and revolution against
oppression?

These are some of the questions that crowd into my
mind as I am launching another book on love. I am not
prepared to answer any of them clearly. To be involved
in the current process of rediscovery or renovation of
love is one thing. To propose an unbiassed assessment of
the dynamics of this process would be another project.
Yet I suspect that a hesitant and qualified "yes" may be
the proper answer to those questions.

One point is certain. A new book on love needs no
apology. A book is justified by what it does and what it
is. It needs no other apology than itself as it is shaped by
its method and filled with its contents. A book on love is
justified by love. All that need be said here is that this
book, several years in the making, has been written and
re-written a few times. Its basic ideas were the object of a
seminar given at Mount Mercy—now Carlow—College
in Pittsburgh, Pennsylvania in the 1960s. They also provided the substance of a series of lectures on love deliv-
ered at the World Center of Liturgical Studies in Florida
in February 1970. This study has taken final shape thanks
to a sabbatical year from the Methodist Theological
School in Ohio.

My investigation is made of two complementary en-
quiries. Or, if one prefers, it joins together two converging approaches. Part One is more analytical, and Part
Two is more synthetic. Part One leads from the philosophy of love of the ancient Greeks, through biblical reflections, to a religious philosophy of the self. Part Two
continues with a biblical study of some key concepts,
which lead to viewing the mysteries of the incarnation
and of the Trinity as mysteries of the divine love. To

these two parts I have added a final chapter. This relates
the previous inquiries to contemporary concerns about
the social-political dimensions of Christian love.

I have read and, I hope, digested, much of the literature on love, both ancient and modern. But I have
avoided extensive bibliographies and have reduced to a
minimum references to other authors. The bibliography
is by no means exhaustive.* But my purpose was not to
take a survey of past or present research and theories. It
was to arrive at an understanding of love that would take
account of both its human experience and its divine
dimension. I believe that these two aspects of love are
one, and that this oneness may provide Christians with a
better vantage-point for understanding other religions,
including the religion of those who have no religion, yet
who do experience love in their heart.

This volume ought to be read as a companion piece to
some previous publications, especially *The Church Tomorrow* (New York: Herder and Herder, 1965), *The Pilgrim Church* (New York: Herder and Herder, 1967),
Meditation on the Word (New York: Paulist, 1968), *La Religion à l'epreuve des idées modernes* (Paris: Centurion, 1970).
It expresses the same basic concerns, and it carries them
a few steps further.

Unless otherwise indicated, biblical quotations are
taken from the New American Bible.

*See Bibliographical Note, p. 159

PART I

The Structure of Love

I

Tragic Love

The focus of most current theological research is anthropological. Theology studies man, seeks for a method in the human sciences, and sees the problems of man as its basic concerns. Such an emphasis was needed after the metaphysical and the historical trends of the entire Christian past. Yet there remains considerable hesitancy as to the proper features of a theological anthropology. A few remarks about the assumptions and presuppositions of my approach will therefore not be out of place.[1]

Whereas theological attention is now shifting, I take it for granted that the structure of theological thought remains stable. For this structure is embedded in the realities of revelation and salvation, in the requirements of rationality, and in the cumulative data of experience. Human reason and its scientific achievements are not the source of theological insight: this is the Christian experience of faith seeking intellection. Deeply personal, this experience rests on gifts from the Spirit rather than on human capabilities. For this reason, theologians will rely, not only on their own experience, but above all on that of others as recorded in the Christian tradition. The Scriptures will be the starting point and a permanent frame of reference. The chief artisans and witnesses of the Christian past, as they reflected on Scripture, on previous tradition and on their experience and on that of their contemporaries, will be kept in mind constantly. The future, and the concepts of eschatology and of hope which are radically related to it, will inspire goals and purposes. From the present age, which has opened anthropology as a scientific field, theologians will draw the urge to reflect, more often than was the case previously, on themselves as human beings.

What is central to the experience of being human? The rise of political theologies, of politically oriented liberation theologies, of secularization theologies, and of politically motivated theologies of hope, suggests that man, as creator of the *polis*, as society-builder, should be at the center of theological anthropology. In my *Woman in Christian Tradition* (Notre Dame, 1973) I have suggested on the contrary that the relationship between man and woman ought to be at the center of theological anthropology. For the woman-man relationship is the most basic of all human interrelationships and the one most immediately open to the divine dimension. I therefore intend to study one aspect of the woman-man relationship, namely the structure of love.

I could begin with a confidential self-analysis and explain how I experience love and how I relate to women in general and to some women in particular. But, to say nothing of the distaste I feel at the idea of public exposure, I do not believe that one could learn much from such an existential approach. Contemporary man—be that myself or another—can hardly provide the light that will illumine him. He rather gives us a datum for reflection, upon which the classical loci of Christian wisdom, Scripture, and the tradition, should throw their light. What we need is to re-read the Scriptures with our anthropological concerns in mind.

The concern for theological anthropology is by no

means new. For that matter, historical research has persuaded me that hardly anything is ever new in theology. New foci and new emphases rarely create new structures and new contents. In fact, our current problems and concerns have been anticipated by previous trends of our civilization, both in the Western world and in humanity in general. We are not the first to raise the problem of love. This was a major topic of theological reflection in the twelfth and the seventeenth centuries, and Kierkegaard examined it at length in the nineteenth.[2] Besides, love was a subject matter for systematic thought long before the Christian era. Some reflections on pre-Christian conceptions will help us to focus our problem and to assess the Christian tradition.

◆ ◆ ◆ ◆ ◆

It is still fairly commonplace among students of comparative religions to think that universal love as taught by Jesus belongs to the patrimony of all religious prophets. Indeed many religions, and not least those of the Far East, teach universal love. But is universal love the same in all religions?

For clarity's sake my remarks in answer to this question will be centered on Buddhism, which does teach universal love, identified with universal compassion.[3] Compassion is the solidarity in misery of all beings caught in the wheel of suffering. Suffering itself derives from desire. Therefore nothing should be desired. The good life should be reached, not by desire, but by abstaining from desire. This follows logically from the eight fundamental truths of the Buddhist faith. First, all creatures are caught in the wheel of suffering; second, suffering comes from desire which cannot be fulfilled; third, desire derives from lack of self-control; fourth, lack of self-control comes from ignorance. We suffer because we desire; we desire because we do not control ourselves; we do not control ourselves because we are ignorant of the root of suffering. But the process may be reversed by acquiring knowledge. This is not intellectual or scientific knowledge, but ethical knowledge: the knowledge of the right way of life. Such knowledge inspires self-control, which suppresses desire, and absence of desire stifles suffering.[4]

The twofold wheel of suffering and of overcoming suffering throws light on the nature of Buddhist compassion. Who suffers, desires, lacks self-control, is ignorant? Who acquires knowledge, acquires self-control, renounces desire, ceases to suffer? According to Buddhist philosophy, a human being is not a person in the Western sense of the term; he is not a center of awareness which remains continuous with itself; he is not a stable individual. Human consciousness is only an aggregate of psychic phenomena; it is a catena of constellations of happenings with no permanent center. The self is not the body, the mind, the soul; it is what remains after the body, the mind, the soul have been eliminated. The self is therefore not being; it is void, emptiness, nonbeing, the peace of absence. To know this is the supreme knowledge, the true identity, which is represented mystically as "Buddhahood," as participation in the nonbeing of the Buddha. When suffering has been lost, human beings discover their own nonexistence. The result is peace, nirvana. But this is not achieved in a day. And what does one do while true knowledge is sought? This is precisely the place of compassion. We ought to feel compassion for all creatures that are caught in the wheel, that have no knowledge, no self-control, who desire and who suffer. Such compassion need not entail subjective or emotional involvement. It should itself be free from desire, especially the desire to love. It should reach all who suffer, who are knowledgeless, who have not voided their self.

Caught in ignorance, all creatures deserve compassion. Animals, women, men, deserve to be pitied. Such pity is universal. It includes the positive aspect of zeal for the end of suffering, for the enlightenment of all who suffer. Yet this zeal is without passion. It is an objective, detached judgment that all need to be saved from positivity. Yet it also entails a missionary endeavor to convert, to help people realize the basic truths. This missionary zeal has inspired a model of holiness with the image and ideal of the *bodhisattva*, who chooses to delay his own nirvana in order to preach conversion to others. The saint places his salvation after that of all creatures.

Although such a conception is attractive, it hardly corresponds to the standard understanding of love in Christianity. Yet it has not been without some influence on Christian authors who have examined the nature of love. In *The Tragic Sense of Life*, Miguel de Unamuno writes:

> The most tragic thing in the world and in life is love. Love is the child of illusion and the parent of illusion. Love is consolation in desolation. It is the sole medicine against death for it is death's brother.

> Pity is the essence of human spiritual love, of the love that is conscious of being love, of the love that is not purely animal, of the love in a world of a rational person. Love pities, and pities most when it loves most.

> We pity what is like ourselves, and the greater and the clearer the sense of our likeness, the greater our pity.[5]

While Unamuno wrote in Spain, in the context of a slightly heterodox personal view of Christianity, an

American author who may be described as post-
Christian writes this poem:*

> There is no way to lose.
> If there was a way
> then
> when sun is shining on pond
> and I go West, thou East,
> which one does the true sun
> follow?
> Which one does the true one borrow
> since neither one is the true one,
> there is no true one way.
> And the sun is a delusion
> of a way multiplied by two
> and multiplied millionfold.
> Since there is no way, no Buddhas,
> no Dharmas, no conceptions,
> only One Ecstasy
> and Right Mindedness
> is mindfulness
> that the way is No-way
> anyhow Sameway
> then what am I to do
> beyond writing this instructive
> poesy, ride a magic carpet
> of self ecstasy, or wait
> for death like the children
> in the Funeral Street after
> the black bus has departed
> or what?[6]

Here, Jack Kerouac expresses the feeling of total emptiness. He speaks of himself and his post-Christian despair. But he also speaks of all creatures, and then the
feeling of emptiness becomes universal compassion.

*Copyright©by Jack Kerouac. Reprinted by permission of The Ster-
ling Lord Agency, Inc.

◆ ◆ ◆ ◆ ◆

The Christian experience of love has been influenced by
the ancient Greeks, chiefly in keeping with the two approaches instanced by Plato and Aristotle.[7]

The details of Plato's doctrine could be discussed at
length. Yet one point is generally accepted. As described
in *The Banquet*, love is a way of ascent to "the great ocean
of beauty" where, by contemplation, a man becomes "a
friend of God and immortal if any man ever is."[8] The
ascent begins with sexual love, which derives from the
cosmic longing of the human race to recover its original
unity. The desire "to be united and melted together with
the beloved and to become one from two" comes from
the presence of an androgynous archetype in the deep
recesses of the human soul. Namely, humankind as we
know it would result from a primitive split. Once "we
were one whole," male and female as one being. Now
we still long for our original state of oneness: "The desire
for the whole and the pursuit of it is named love."[9]
Sexual love searches for a lost partnership with a being of
the other sex with whom we would be one if mankind
had not been split by some kind of original fall or sin. For
Plato, however, who places this account of love in the
mouth of Aristophanes, there is also another type of
love. Above and beyond the "common love," which
joins bodies in the quest of original unity, a "heavenly or
uranian love" associates souls together in a search for
heavenly beauty.[10] In *The Banquet*, the ascent to heavenly
beauty begins with the contemplation of a beautiful male
body. Freed from entanglement with females, the male
lover of beauty rises gradually from the beauty of the
body to the beauty of the soul and from there to the
purely spiritual beauty of God. Love is *eros*, desire.

The ambiguous elements of Plato's approach, which
appear clearly in the place given to homosexual contem-

plation of bodily beauty, were considerably corrected in
the neo-Platonism of Plotinus. *Eros* is still related to the
perception of beauty. It is an ecstasy caused by the admi-
ration of beauty:

> Such emotion all beauty should induce—an astonish-
> ment, a delicious wonderment, a longing, a love, a trem-
> bling that is all delight. It may be felt for things invisible
> quite as for things you see, and indeed the soul does feel it.
> All souls, we can say, feel it, but souls that are apt for love
> feel it especially. It is the same as with bodily beauty. All
> perceive it. Not all are stung by it. Only those we call lovers
> ever are.[11]

Love is *eros.* It aspires to rise above itself to oneness with
another, and, beyond all, with the one whom Plotinus
calls the One. It is in this purified form that the doctrines
of the Platonists passed into Christianity in the third and
fourth centuries after Christ: the desire for God is the
most basic and also the highest form of human love.

◆ ◆ ◆ ◆ ◆

Aristotle describes love in books 8 and 9 of his *Ethics.* We
are far from Plato's graduated program of contemplation. *Philia* rather than *eros* is at the center. *Philia*
corresponds to friendship. It is the mutual esteem that
friends have for one another. No one can live without it.
Yet Aristotle proposes a largely mercantile conception of
friendship: this is an agreement prompted by the pleasure that friends find in their mutual presence and con-
versation, by the profit to be gained from association,
and by common interests. Friendship is fed by profit,
and it is associated with experience of the good, the
pleasant, and the useful.

Accordingly there are three kinds of friendship, motivated respectively by the good (moral friendship), by the
pleasant (esthetic friendship) and by the useful (business

friendship). These relationships develop best among equals. Given the structure of Greek society at the time of Aristotle, this rules out friendship between men and women. Yet friendship among men or women of un-equal rank is still possible, as long as the low-class person brings to it more than the high-class person. This extra contribution is necessary so that no one should lower himself through friendship. Then an artificial equality is created among unequal persons. *Philia* as partnership is then possible.

Yet Aristotle corrects his own conception. For he also describes a friend as "a second self"; as "one who desires and performs the good, or what appears to him to be the good, of another for the sake of that other"; as "one who desires the existence and preservation of his friend for the friend's sake"; as "one who has the same ideals"; as "one who shares the joys and sorrows of his friend." Accordingly, *philia* includes an element of self-forgetfulness balanced by commitment to the good of another person. Why should anyone forget self for a friend? Aristotle correlates friendship and self-dignity. The descriptions I have quoted constitute the "five marks" of friendship; yet each of these marks "appears also in the feelings which a good man entertains toward himself." Thus *philia* emerges when the feelings that a good person entertains toward self are oriented toward another person. [12]

In Aristotle's perspective there is no trace of *eros* in *philia*. The existence and the experience of *eros* are recognized, when "lovers find their chief delight in gazing upon the beloved and prefer sight to all the other senses, for this is the seat and source of love (*eros*)." [13] In contrast, friends do not get together in order to share the emotional and esthetic delights of contemplating each other's physical, intellectual, and moral beauty. Rather, they share what they like in common, such as drinking, playing games, engaging in athletics, hunting, philosophy. Unlike *eros, philia* does not drive anyone out of self toward another in ecstasy. It reinforces self-centeredness by accenting one's own likes and dislikes in the company of like-minded people. The standard of *philia* is the self.

◆ ◆ ◆ ◆ ◆

A sharp conflict opposes *eros*, the desire to ascend higher through love, and *philia*, the partnership of games and leisure. This conflict may be experienced when *eros* raises us up and *philia* brings us down to the level of our games. Such a conflict is illustrated in the tragedy of Euripides, *The Bacchae. Eros* is symbolized by the orgiastic cult of Dionysus—then, around 407 B.C., in Macedonia, a new religion in which the initiates seek wild ecstasies in hills and woods, far from the settled pace of towns and the ordinary human relations of society.[14] *Philia* is the commonsense background with which *eros* is contrasted and on which some of the disillusioned *bacchae* fall back after discovering that *eros*, in its Dionysian form, was a hideous mistake. The central point made by Euripides, as I understand his work, seems to be that *eros* is ultimately self-destroying: it is destroyed by the longer-lasting inertia of society, by its own reaction to opposition, which tends to be more violent than efficacious, and by its ecstatic blindness. Then, the broken adepts of Dionysus face only two choices: to renounce *eros*, or to adore its divine but cruel mystery.[15]

Yet the dream of reconciliation cannot be completely eliminated. Is Greek tragedy the last word about *eros*? Can one hope that *eros* and *philia*, the uplifting through love and the comradeship of life in society, may still learn to live together and to become, if not complementary partners, at least associates?

♦ ♦ ♦ ♦ ♦

The conception of love as *eros* influenced the Christian mystics' search for total love. The conception of love as acquisitive friendship influenced the Christian theologians' construction of ethical systems of behavior. Christian reflection about love has thus tended to waver between Plato and Aristotle, between love as ecstasy and love as appropriation. In ecstatic love I escape the boundaries of my self; I am thrown into the life and being of another whom I cherish more than myself; I fall into the abyss of the infinite discovery of God. However, fearing the distortions of ecstatic love by guilt (the *concupiscentia* of St. Augustine and the scholastics) Christian theologians have distrusted ecstatic love, especially between men and women. They have struggled to moderate its ecstasy with carefully elaborated control systems called virtues. They have even looked askance at the ecstatic love of God, which is unable to speak the clear language of the Schools and is forced, in order to express itself, into profound but obscure symbolisms. They have therefore tried to channel all love into a moderate form of acquistiveness, in which prudence and justice hold in check the appropriating instinct.[16] Appropriating love takes what I need in another human person. A marriage agreement entitles me to the body of another. Western society has traditionally been based on this sort of contractual justice. Yet such a system fosters its own destruction. For the acquistive way of life encourages competition between the holders of rights, and it fosters conflicting claims. This is particularly destructive in relation to God. For God owes nothing to anyone but himself. He gives the whole of his being in love to his creatures, and he can be adequately answered only by unrestricted self-giving. In relation to human love, acquisi-

tive love is a fertile ground for both moral and psychological guilt: it tends to undermine the integrity of those
who are caught in it, making each person, whether in
Aristotle's friendship or in contractual sex, an object to
be seized by another.

It comes as no surprise, then, that Greek tragedy has
survived in the Christian experience of love. Classical
Christianity has in fact maintained a fatal dualism. Acquisitive love has been hallowed as the normal pattern
for marriage: a male acquires a female for his gratification
and service, and the female accepts her part of this contract for the sake of security, motherhood, and occasional sexual pleasure. One may recognize here the first
"goods" of matrimony in the theology of St. Augustine:
proles (procreation) and *fides* (mutual covenant), which
the third good, *sacramentum* (the sacramental seal), attempts with doubtful success to deprive of their most
abrasive acquisitiveness.

Ecstatic love, which the Greeks experienced, according to their taste, in Platonic contemplation and in intellectual and sexual intercourse with *hetairai* (high-class
harlots), was channelled by Christianity into the contemplative life.[17] Shunning the entanglements of marriage, men and women have sought God in solitude and
explored the ways of oneness with their transcendent
Creator who, in the Lord Incarnate, makes himself their
eternal lover through the Holy Spirit. The mingling of
these two loves, human and divine, has remained a
somewhat eccentric phenomenon, as it has been dis-
couraged by the institutionalization of the contemplative
life in monastic foundations and by the mandatory celi-
bacy of the Latin clergy.

A dichotomy has thus grown between the lay life,
normally lived in marriage as an institution of acquisitive
love, and the consecrated life, normally lived in monastic

seclusion or in the official service of the Christian community. In our times this dichotomy has reached the
proportions of a catastrophe, as the lay life, unduly cut
off from the depths of the Spirit, has been increasingly
secularized, and the consecrated life, unduly closed to
the full range of human relationships, has become stif-
ling. The Catholic tradition attempted to bridge the gap
between these two loves and these two ways of life by
consecrating marriage as a sacrament. [18] The relationship
of husband and wife was oriented thereby toward companionship in the service of God and neighbor. Yet the
basic difficulty has remained: a life based on physical
possession between a man and a woman naturally reinforces self-centeredness instead of leading to the death
and resurrection of the self in the love of God. The
sacramentality of marriage implies its permanence. But
acquisitive love, in regard to sex as in other areas, invites
competition. Thus, far from converging with the ecstatic
love of God, marriage, despite its sacramental form, has
fallen victim to acquisitive sexual love. Both the breakdown of marriage and the deliquescence of religious
orders can be traced to the radical conflict between acquisitive and ecstatic love.

In human experience, life without some kind of love
leads to a loneliness that fosters despair. But which is the
way of love that overcomes loneliness? Is it the impulse
to appropriate the pleasant, the good, and the useful
which we discover in fellow human persons? If I am
male, is it the acquisitive love that urges me to possess a
wife? If I am female, is it yielding to the possessive love of
a husband? In either case, I live off the substance of
another, and I run the risk of swelling my egotism by
devouring my partner.

Is the love that overcomes loneliness a deep urge toward divine beauty, an *eros* that elevates human per-

sons beyond themselves into a realm of spiritual freedom and creativity in common with others? Should not sexual loving between woman and man be, not the basis or the purpose of mutual commitment, but the fruition of a spiritual convergence toward the holy, the fullness of self-giving when a man and a woman have already given their selves to God in ecstatic love?

We are powerfully tempted today to bypass the questions thus raised by our Greek heritage. We may be persuaded, or we may simply hope, listening to scores of false prophets, that the Asian perspective may open a way of escape. But can there be true fulfillment if love must ultimately pour our lost selves into the void of nonbeing behind the misleading appearance of illusory being? Can the hunger of men and women for true life be satisfied by a brotherhood-sisterhood of suffering in which all share a deep mutual compassion before the final dissolution of their selves?

Notes

1. For a thorough discussion of theological method, see my *La Théologie parmi les sciences humaines* (Paris: Beauchesne, 1975).

2. For a list of twelfth-century authors who have dealt with the question, see Etienne Gilson, *La Théologie mystique de saint Bernard* (Paris: Vrin, 1974), pp. 15–16; the classical study of this medieval movement is Pierre Rousselot, *Pour l'histoire du problème de l'amour au moyen age* (Münster: Aschendorffsche Buchhandlung, 1908). The seventeenth-century discussion was centered on "Quietism" and the spirituality of Fénelon; see François Varillon, *Fénelon et le pur amour* (Paris: Seuil, 1957); Tavard, *La Tradition au XVIIe siècle* (Paris: Le Cerf, 1969). The thought of Kierkegaard will be found in many of his works, chiefly in *Either/Or* and in *Works of Love*.

3. The idea that all religions are one in their advocacy of love as the basic ethical and religious principle is assumed by Pitirim Sorokin, *The Ways and Power of Love* (Boston: Beacon, 1954). For a discussion of the Buddhist form of love from a Christian standpoint, see Henri de

Lubac, *Aspects of Buddhism*, trans. George Lamb (New York: Sheed & Ward, 1954). In his volume, *Christianity and the Encounter of World Religions* (New York: Columbia University Press, 1963), Paul Tillich identifies Buddhist and Christian love, but the accuracy of his knowledge of Buddhism is questionable.

4. See the discussion of pain in *The Questions of King Milinda*, ed. Max Miller, Vol. 1, Sacred Books of the East, Vol. 35 (New York: Verry, 1963), pp. 190–95.

5. Miguel de Unamuno, *The Tragic Sense of Life*, trans. J.E. Crawford Flitch (New York: Dover, 1954), pp. 132, 137, 141.

6. Jack Kerouac, *Mexico City Blues* (New York: Grove, 1959), 226 Chorus, p. 228.

7. For a good, nontechnical discussion of Plato and Aristotle, see Pedro Laín Entralgo, *Sobre la Amistad* (Madrid: Revista de Occidente, 1972), pp. 19–33. His interpretation differs from mine. This book adds a good presentation of Cicero, who mediated Greek conceptions to the Christian West by way of Augustine; see pp. 35–50.

8. This is from Diotima's speech to Socrates, in *Great Dialogues of Plato*, trans. Rouse (New York: NAL, 1956), pp. 105–06.

9. This is from the speech of Aristophanes at the banquet, *ibid.*, p. 88.

10. This is from the speech of Pausanias at the banquet, *ibid.*, p. 78.

11. Plotinus, *Ennead I*, Elmer O'Brien, ed., *The Essential Plotinus* (New York: NAL, 1964), p. 38.

12. Aristotle, *Ethics* (Baltimore: Penguin, 1963), bk. 9, ch. 4, pp. 266–67.

13. *Ibid.*, bk. 9, ch. 12, p. 284.

14. For the context of religious movements in Greece, see Martin Nilsson, *Greek Piety* (New York: Norton, 1969).

15. Euripides, *The Bacchae* (also called *The Bacchantes*), in Great Books of the Western World, ed. Robert Hutchins and Mortimer Adler (Chicago: Encyclopedia Britannica, 1952), Vol. 5, pp. 340–52.

16. In Anders Nygren's analysis (*Agape and Eros* [Philadelphia: Westminster, 1953], p. 449–664) *caritas* emerges, from St. Augustine to the scholastics and later Catholic conceptions of love as the sanctification of acquisitiveness. This analysis is marred by the assimilation of ecstatic love, *eros*, to acquisitiveness, and the rejection of it as a Christian form of love. See below, Chapter 6, for further remarks on Nygren's theories. In another perspective, the Marxist critique of traditional marriage is based on its identification with the acquisition of a woman as a man's private property. Friedrich Engels initiated this critique in *The Origin of the Family, Private Property and the State* (1884).

See August Bebel, *Woman Under Socialism*, trans. Daniel de Leon (New York: Schochen, 1971).

17. In *Die Frau in der antiken Welt und im Urchristentum* (Leipzig: Koehler und Amelang, 1955), Johannes Leipoldt makes the intriguing suggestion that the first Christian communities of celibate consecrated women were the historical successors to the Greek *gynecaeum* and the oriental *harem*, minus the male master. Christian mystics have seen a symbolic relation between the sexual life and the contemplative life. But the tantric traditions of some forms of Indian and Tibetan religion, which have seen a direct relationship between sex and contemplation, deserve investigation. Such an investigation remains difficult in the context of the Judeo-Christian biblical heritage, on account of the prophets' opposition to Canaanite rites, which included sacred prostitution. On Charles Williams's understanding of "being in love" as the ecstatic perception of divine glory in a human person, see Mary McDermot Shideler, *The Theology of Romantic Love: An Analysis of the Writings of Charles Williams* (Grand Rapids, Mich., Eerdmans, 1962). See the next chapter for my understanding of the Song of Songs and its sexual symbolism.

18. On the sacramentality of marriage, see Edward Schillebeeckx: *Christians Marriage, Human Reality and Saving Mystery* (New York: Sheed & Ward, 1965).

II

Ethical Love

The ethical core and the doctrinal structure of the Jewish experience of God are contained in the great passage of Deuteronomy which follows the traditional prayer, *Shema' Israel:*

> Hear, o Israel! The Lord is our God, the Lord alone! Therefore, you shall love the Lord, your God, with all your heart, and with all your soul, and with all your strength. Take to heart these words which I enjoin on you today. Drill them into your children. Speak of them at home and abroad, whether you are busy or at rest. Bind them at your wrist as a sign and let them be as a pendant on your forehead. Write them on the doorposts of your houses and on your gates (Deut. 6:4–9).

Doctrinally, this profession of faith glorifies the oneness and the uniqueness of God. Ethically, it states the law of love. To speak of "the Lord, your God," is to bind God and man together in an intimate relationship in which man is invited to grow unrestrictedly.

This word is addressed to Israel as a community. And it applies to individual members of the People insofar as each identifies himself with the whole Israel. The love in which Israel shares is experienced as fellowship. Love of God incorporates a person into the holy community and places him along the chain of the holy tradition. Cemented by the love of God, the community of the elect is two-dimensional: it reaches from past to future (tradition looking forward to its fulfillment); and it implies mutual presence here and now in the light of the felt love of God (the People of God as an earthly community). It follows that love as a human experience among the members of the community cannot be reduced to personal relationships of intimacy; rather, it grows out of the divine commandment as a concretion of the corporate love binding the community together.[1]

Precisely, the Ten Commandments are modes of determination of the basic love of God. The motivation of revealing the commandments is God's love for mankind:

> I, the Lord, your God, am a jealous God, inflicting punishment for their fathers' wickedness on the children of those who hate me, down to the third and fourth generation, but bestowing mercy, down to the thousandth generation, on the children of those who love me and keep my commandments (Deut. 5:9–10).

The punishment of the wicked reaches those who, in the tribal family, effectively carry out the wicked orders of the elderly group leader. For those who love him, God's attitude knows no bounds. His benevolence is not limited to the living but it will outlast all those now alive and be felt by their faraway descendants.

The basis for the Old Testament concept and practice of love is therefore simple: love as a human attitude means love for God but it implies also the practice of justice among mankind. In principle, the structure of society distinguishes among three categories, the members of the People, the peaceful alien, and the enemy alien. Each person defines himself in relation to the others in answer to the question, Who is my neighbor?

The wrath of God is the aspect of divine love that

sinners experience. The struggles of Israel through the ages, the genocide of the ten tribes, the Babylonian captivity, the hardships of the postexilic resettlement, the wars with the Greeks, the Roman colonization, are tokens of divine love. Love expressed as wrath is directed against unfaithful Israel and idolaters. The theological explanation of the wars of Israel extols God's love, which men and women experience differently according to their faithful or unfaithful, believing or idolatrous mental and moral attitude.

The prophets of Israel opened up a broad universalism in religion and in ethics.[2] God also loves and guides good pagans. Eventually, God's Messiah will bring all nations to obey Torah and to worship at Jerusalem. Hatred for the People's enemies, identified as God's enemies, remains conditional. For, except in the oldest strata of the Elias cycle and the prophetic tradition that followed it, the struggle against enemies aims at their repentance and conversion. The alien who converts to God becomes neighbor; and there are notable instances of high-placed Hebrews who are, by blood, of other ethnicities. Aliens who accept the God of Israel force the Hebrews to a reconversion of attitude toward them.

The concept itself of the neighbor derives from the idea and ideal that the People should pattern their behavior on that of God. "Since I, the Lord, brought you up from the land of Egypt that I might be your God, you shall be holy, because I am holy" (Lev. 11:45). God's holiness takes the double form of the awesome, fascinating, fathomless mystery experienced by all the mystics, and of a warm presence of love felt by those whom God favors. God's love implies pity, compassion, sympathy, condescension; it is grace and assistance but also wrath and punishment. It is universal. Human love is also potentially universal, because it is patterned on divine love. It is ethical, since it is grounded in a clear notion of good and evil as formulated in Torah. One should love God and hate evil, love those who do good and hate those who practice evil. The actual form of God's love for each human person will be conditioned by the form of human love.

Besides love for the neighbor or universal love, the Old Testament also refers to friendship or selective love. Admittedly, Judaism never gave friendship the central place it was granted in classical Hellenism. Yet an interesting paradigm of friendship is presented in the Books of Samuel in reference to David and Jonathan.

> By the time David finished speaking with Saul, Jonathan had become as fond of David as if his life depended on him; he loved him as he loved himself . . . And Jonathan entered into a bond with David, because he loved him as himself. Jonathan divested himself of the mantle he was wearing and gave it to David, along with his military dress, and his sword, his bow and his belt (1 Sam. 18:1–4).

This type of love entails a high degree of commitment to the other person, to the point that Jonathan identifies his own self, his *nephesh*, with that of David. Although Jonathan's father, Saul, eventually wants to destroy David, Jonathan is raised by friendship above the interests of his own clan so that he protects David from his father. The final redaction of 1 Sam. 20 suggests that God is also involved in their friendship:

> At length Jonathan said to David: "Go in peace in keeping with what we two have sworn by the name of the Lord: 'The Lord shall be between you and me, and between your posterity and mine for ever' " (1 Sam. 20:42).

Such a friendship has a religious dimension. It is as strong and as binding as an oath taken in God's name. When both Saul and Jonathan fall in battle, David mourns, for the one as his king, for the other as his soul-friend:

> Saul and Jonathan, beloved and cherished, separated neither in life nor in death, swifter than eagles, stronger than lions! . . . I grieve for you, Jonathan my brother! most dear have you been to me; more precious have I held love for you than love for women (2 Sam. 1:23, 26).

This love is notably different from the universal love for the neighbor enjoined on the whole community, although it is the same word, 'ahab, that is used in both cases. The commandment is universal. Friendship is selective. The former is general; the latter is specific. The former regulates behavior toward society; the latter unites persons to persons in their singularities. The one fulfills an obligation; the other freely binds friends together above and beyond all legal obligations, and more deeply than any law can enjoin.

◆ ◆ ◆ ◆ ◆

Love for the neighbor and selective friendship do not exhaust the Old Testament experience. Several of the prophets compare God's love for Israel with a man's love for his fiancée or his wife. The comparison is both positive and negative: although God loves Israel as his bride, Israel has behaved like an adultress and a prostitute. In an indefinite future, however, contingent on Israel's repentance, God will love his bride again as he did formerly in the desert. This theme is vividly illustrated by Hosea's marriage to "a harlot wife" (Hos. 1–3). It is used with powerful effect by Isaiah (Isa. 1:21), Jeremiah (Jer. 2:1), Ezekiel (Ezek. 16; 23), II Isaiah (Isa. 54:6).

Yet the negative theme of Israel's infidelity is contrasted with the true love of God wooing Israel back to himself, not with Israel's loving fidelity to God in the covenant of a beautiful marital relationship. Although this may not be far from the thought of the prophets, none of them really attempts to see the beauty of Israel's marriage to God from the side of Israel. Perhaps it would have been ultimately impossible to describe Israel's tie to God on the pattern of the best relationship between woman and man when oneness of the flesh expresses and deepens total unity of mind and soul. Perhaps also the prophets were hampered by the propensity of biblical literature as a whole—which presumably reflects the mores of the People—to treat the man-woman relationship in a satirical or in a light vein, rarely in depth and with seriousness. This may not be surprising, given the generality of average human experience, in a collection of writings illustrative of the life and self-understanding of a people over many centuries. Obviously, sex was experienced by the Hebrews and the Jews at several qualitatively different levels of purity and awareness.

In Genesis 2:19–24, Adam seeks in *eros* for a companion in whom he hopes to find the same divine glory that is present in himself. The answer to his *eros* is the creation of woman. In her, Adam recognizes God's beauty. It is significant that later meditations on creation, such as those of Ps. 8:4–10 or of Ben Sirach (Ecclus.) 17:1–18, identify the image of God in man as the reflection of divine beauty. It is beauty that is loved by a man when he unites himself to another in friendship or when he joins himself to a woman as one flesh.

The patriarchs are polygamous. Jealousy reigns among their wives. Concubines are used for sex, especially when their mistress is old or sterile. Real love and companionship may unite Abraham and Sarah, Isaac and Rebekah, Jacob and Rachel. Yet Abraham also uses the slave-girl Agar, before throwing her out at Sarah's pleading; Jacob, who already has two wives, takes several concubines from among his wives' slaves; the two daughters of Lot sleep with him when he is drunk because they despair of finding legitimate husbands. Stories of rape and incest abound. By and large, women fulfill two tasks: they serve as means of exchange and alliance between clans, and they bear children.

With their gradual organization as a people, the Hebrews abandoned patriarchal customs. New laws were made, about the taboos of pregnancy and birth, of menstrual blood and seminal liquid. Incest and adultery were defined and prohibited. The penalty for raping a virgin was specified. But if legislation provides a framework for social life, it cannot explain motivations or emotions. It gives no indication of the philosophy underlying taboos and regulations. Far less does it measure the quality of true love as experienced among friends or between a man and a woman.

According to the historical books, the kings led a chaotic sex life. David has wives and concubines; and his passion for Uriah's wife is dwelt upon. Amnon rapes his half-sister Tamar. Absalom challenges his father David's authority by sleeping with David's concubines. Solomon keeps an abundant harem, "seven hundred wives of princely rank and three hundred concubines" (1 Kings 11:3). On the whole, these records constitute a sad commentary on the man-woman relationship in the higher strata of Hebraic society. They hardly help us to assess the higher meaning of love for the Old Testament.

Other writings of a different nature may help us to obtain a better insight. The books of Ruth and of Tobit illustrate marriage customs of different periods. Ruth throws light on the law of the levirate, tied to polygamy, by which a childless widow was entitled to marry her husband's nearest relative (Deut. 25:5–10). Tobit illustrates the problems of endogamic marriage, by which wives are to be found within the clan rather than outside

(Gen. 24). It also describes some superstitions concerning the power of demons over sexual unions, and it teaches a magic way of driving the demon away. Yet both Ruth and Tobit point to the delicacy of human love, if not as an image of God's love (this perspective does not surface here), at least as a way of life in fidelity to the Torah and to God's love.

Proverbs contains folk wisdom about women. It urges young men to avoid alien women and prostitutes. A wife is her husband's property, a well into which he should pour all his waters (Prov. 5:15–19). The ideal woman of Proverbs 21 is the perfect companion entirely devoted to the service of her household and to the comfort and prestige of her husband. The advice given by Ben Sirach is, likewise, very cautious (Ecclus. 9:1–9; 23:22–27; 25:13–26:18; 36:21–27): women, generally speaking, are not to be trusted; yet a good wife is priceless while a loose woman is a curse. In any case, relationship with women is a matter of common sense and practical wisdom, not of love. The perspective of these books of wisdom is monogamous. But love has nothing to do with marriage. This is a bargain, and a man should strike the best possible one, acquire the least cumbersome, the least talkative, and the most obedient of women, without expecting too much from her. For Qoheleth, who expects nothing from life, the only pleasures are eating and drinking (Eccles. 9:7). As to human love, Qoheleth is quite negative (Eccles. 7:26–28). He recommends enjoying woman, for such things do not last after death (9:9), but this has nothing to do with love.

Like other insights of the Mosaic and prophetic traditions, the possibilities of human love as a terrestrial image of divine love were dimmed in the prophetless centuries that followed the return from the exile and the rebuilding of Jerusalem. The perspective on love is restricted to God's condescending love for the just and to man's love for God as manifested in obedience and in the meditation of Torah.

◆ ◆ ◆ ◆ ◆

With the Song of Songs another perspective is opened.[3] Of uncertain date, of uncertain origin, though it probably drew its inspiration from the same Egypt-oriented court circles as the wisdom books, the Song of Songs is closer to the prophetic books in its positive evaluation of the man-woman relationship. But whereas the prophets celebrate the love of God for Israel, of which the man-woman love can be no more than symbolic, the Song sings of love between man and woman.

Admittedly, there are conflicting interpretations of the book. Song of Songs is an Hebraic expression meaning the most beautiful of all songs. But what is it about? Does the Song proclaim the beauty of sexual longing and experience? Does it lyricize and dramatize the history of Israel's stormy relationship with God as her bridegroom, on the model of the prophetic literature? Does it describe the mystical encounter between God and the soul? One may also ask: Is the Song a coherent lyric poem (or rather a coherent piece of lyrical prose)? Is it a drama destined to be sung and danced? Is it a disparate collection of erotic poetry? Is it a series of wedding songs?

At any rate, what the Song describes is not the love for the neighbor of the older biblical writings. That the Song contains erotic passages does not solve the problem. For in all religions erotic images have symbolized the search of the soul for God and their meeting in nudity of spirit. Even if the Song was intended primarily to be a piece of eroticism, this would at least imply that the sexual expression of *eros* was filled with enough religious meaning to be considered inspired so that the Song could be included among the *Ketubhim* (the "writings") of the Bible.[4] If the Song has a primary mystical intent, or if a mystical dimension may be read into it without distorting the text, then the love of God and erotic love can be so harmonized that the one expresses the other.

I find it helpful to read the Song of Songs as a lyrical dialogue, occasionally interrupted and explained by a chorus, between a man and a woman who love each other. Dialogue must be taken in a broad sense, since it is in reality a succession of monologues in which each sings about the other. The special point is that the love that is described here is both spiritual and sexual. The beauty of each is painted by the other with deep sexual awareness. Yet, while this erotic language is filled with sexual content, it is also symbolic of a profoundly religious dimension: *eros* itself bears the mark of God. "For stern as death is love, relentless as the nether world is devotion; its flames are a blazing fire" (Song, 8:6). In the perspective of the Song, the beauty of the bride seen by the bridegroom, and that of the bridegroom seen by the bride, are themselves divine beauty. Far from opposing body and spirit, the biblical philosophy unites them as forming one flesh. The totality of man and woman is engaged in their mutual love. Flesh loves and flesh is loved in such a reciprocity that each is inseparably subject and object. The flesh of the lovers is body and spirit and is imbued with the Spirit of God. Sex does not rule the relationship. Spirit expresses the intense longing of two persons for each other through the aching of their minds and bodies, and it fulfills this longing in sexual union. The conjunction of spiritual unity with sexual unity in love is the dominant theme of the Song of Songs.

Related to this basic point one finds a literarily more subdued idea, which indicates the ultimate meaning of *eros:* erotic love draws its beauty precisely from the religious dimension and awareness of man and woman. The chorus points to this as it describes woman's hunger for man in terms of eschatological longing: "If you do not know, o most beautiful among women, follow the tracks of the flock and pasture the young ones near the shepherds' camps" (1:8). The chorus asks unanswerable questions, not unlike the koans of Zen: "How does your lover differ from any other?" (5:9) "Where has your lover gone?" (6:1). The chorus calls the woman "Shulammite" (7:1), a term that suggests the infinite peace that she is going to find. The chorus closes up on the vision of an ascent from the infinity of the desert: "Who is this coming up from the desert, leaning upon her lover?" (8:5) The ascent to the city of peace, Jerusalem, is acted out when the People converge upon it for the Passover, chanting the great *hillel* of the songs of ascent. Jerusalem, where God dwells personally in the Holy of Holies, is the model and goal of the lovers' pilgrimage. Spiritual unity, spiritual peace, spiritual love—the peace of the Sabbath—give meaning and beauty to sexual oneness. The lovers' hunger and thirst for each other concretize their eschatological longing for the true Jerusalem. Sexual congress has no other and no less meaning than their eschatological endeavor to obtain the true Jerusalem.

Insofar as it places sex at the acme of spiritual unity, the Song of Songs is the highest expression of the integrity of love in the Old Testament. The rabbis of the synod of Jamnia at the end of the first century, discussing the already accepted canonicity of the book, may have feared that such a book would be misread as sexual-erotic play. In reality, *eros* is sacred when it expresses the unity of male and female in the totality of their being. It is distorted and sinful when enclosed in the sexual relationship. The total oneness of flesh as body and spirit which *eros* should symbolize is negated by merely sexual relations.

If I understand the Song of Songs correctly, holy *eros* is not necessarily restricted to the matrimonial contract. The Song opens up the ideal possibility of an *eros* in which the divine *agape* is itself experienced by two in one flesh regardless of the accepted ethics of the community. The convergence of two persons, their discovery of divine love in their encounter, the deepening of their mutual relationship, their perception of divine beauty in each other, are not dependent on marriage. The Song of Songs celebrates the spiritual freedom of the man-woman relationship when it is grounded in God and focused on him. Only then can love flower in the unrestricted encounter of two persons in one flesh. While the ethics of the Old Testament enjoin marital fidelity (under penalty of death—but only for the wife!), the inspiration that brings a man and a woman into a relationship of infinite love in God creates a "teleological suspension of the ethical," related to the experience of the glory of God in another human being.

This would seem to be the meaning of the erotic-mystical poetry of the Song of Songs.

◆ ◆ ◆ ◆ ◆

Post-Christian Judaism developed the reflection on love which had been initiated by the biblical authors. The Song of Songs was idealized, being interpreted in a purely mystical sense which did not favor the unity of *eros* as the spirit-flesh love constitutive of the man-woman relationship. In other areas rabbinic reflection constantly reinterpreted the biblical datum, thus making it relevant to successive generations and giving it the further dimension of cumulative tradition. Considerable spiritual advance was undoubtedly made in the contemplation and understanding of divine love.

Growth in understanding may be perceived in the many schools of Jewish mysticism. "You must speak evil of no creatures," Moses Cordovero writes in the sixteenth century, "not even of animals; you must not curse beings, but bless them even in the midst of anger."[5] Love extends beyond the boundaries of the People. It includes all mankind and even all creatures because it unites all beings in the love of God. "The desire and the hope of the just is the Holy One, blessed be he."[6] This is not compassion. It is positive love. One should love all beings, not because they are miserable, but because they are good with the radiance of God's glory.

Even when the centrality of Israel is affirmed as the first in God's choice, every man and even every creature are also reached by God's covenant of love, for Israel designates the People as called to a universal messianic mission.

It is in the perspective of love that the Sabbath should be understood. This is a day of divine love that throws light on the whole week. The liturgy of the Gaon 'Amran prays: "Because of the love you had for your People Israel and because of the compassion you felt, o our King, for the children of your covenant, you gave us, o Lord, our God, the seventh day."[7]

The Jewish mysticism of the land (*ha' eretz*) and of the Holy City should also be understood in this perspective. The land is the concrete testimony of God's love for his People. It embodies promises that go back, in Israel's memory, to the patriarchs of the distant past. Through centuries of diaspora, in the medieval ghettoes, during the pogroms, in the recent persecutions of Jews at the hands of powers of this world, the land of Israel has remained as a focus of hope for Israel's love of God because in the choice of this land God's love had been manifested first:

> If I forget you, Jerusalem,
> may my right hand be forgotten!
> May my tongue cleave to my palate
> if I remember you not,
> if I place not Jerusalem
> ahead of my joy (Ps. 137:5–6).

Jerusalem is the living proof of the priority of God's love and of the power of his prevenient grace.

Above all, the faithful Jew ought to love God. He should be, not "a Pharisee out of fear," but rather "a Pharisee out of love." No less a philosopher than Moses Maimonides places the love of God at the apex of all values:

> When a man loves God with the proper love, he immediately fulfills all the commandments out of love. And what is this proper love? It is to love God with great, extreme, ardent love so that the soul of the lover is tied to the love of God; this love throws him in a state of perpetual torment, like a man who loves a woman and is never free from this love of her but is constantly tormented, whether the lover rests or goes about, and even when he eats and drinks. The perpetual torments of the lovers of God are more intense still. The Scripture commands it: "with all your heart and with all your soul." Solomon expresses it in his metaphorical language: "I am sick with love." The entire Song of Songs is the image of this situation.[9]

Thus, love has been experienced in the Jewish tradition as embodying in itself the heart of human life before God. Life is lived in God's light. It is experienced at its summit as between human persons in the face-to-face relationship of man and woman. It is rooted in the soil of a homeland. It is lived in the succession of days and weeks by the strength of the weekly Sabbath where

God's love is experienced in the liturgies of the home and of the synagogue. The meaning and purpose of life are fully expressed in Torah, the gift of God's love, as God's love for man and as human love for God. The biblical and Jewish tradition tends to the full integration of the many aspects of human and divine love.

Notes

1. On the biblical doctrine of love (*chesed* and *'ahab*) see the commentaries on the prophets, especially on Hosea. Compare with ideas at the time of Jesus, in Joseph Bonsirven, *Le Judäisme Palestinien au temps de Jésus-Christ*, 2 vols. (Paris: Beauchesne, 1934–1935), mainly pp. 43–47 (fear and love of God), 198–206 (the neighbor), 249–280 (duties of charity); available in English: *Palestinian Judaism* (Westminister, Md.: Christian Classics, 1964). See several studies included in John M. Oesterreicher, ed., *The Bridge: Yearbook of Judeo-Christian Studies*, Vol. 4 (New York: Pantheon, 1962); Kathryn Sullivan, "The God of Israel, God of Love," pp. 23–43; Joseph Brenan, "Love of God in the Talmud," pp. 119–48.

2. Abraham J. Heschel, *The Prophets*, 2 vols. (New York: Harper and Row, 1969); E. W. Heaton, *The Old Testament Prophets* (Baltimore: Penguin, 1961).

3. On the Song of Songs I follow largely Daniel Lys, *Le plus beau chant de la création* (Paris: Le Cerf, 1968). See Barry Ulanov, "The Song of Songs: The Rhetoric of Love," in Oesterreicher, *Bridge*, Vol. 4, pp. 89–118.

4. On the synod of Jamnia, where the inclusion of the Song in the Bible was endorsed by a number of rabbis, see Lys, *Le blus beau chant*, pp. 24–27.

5. Quoted in Guy Casaril, *Rabbi Siméon Bar Yochai et la Cabbale* (Paris: Sevil, 1961), p. 143.

6. Quoted in Georges Vajda, *L'Amour de Dieu dans la littérature juive du moyen age* (Paris: Vrin, 1957), p. 56.

7. *Ibid.*, p. 32.

8. *Ibid.*, p. 48.

9. This is from *The Book of Knowledge*, quoted in Vajda, *L'Amour de Dieu*, p. 127. See Abraham Cohen, *The Teachings of Maimonides*, rev. ed. (New York: Ktav, 1969).

III

Universal Love

Who is my neighbor? When the New Testament enjoins the disciples of Jesus to love their enemies, it clearly includes enemies among the neighbors who are to be loved like one's own self. Are these enemies national or personal? The question arises from the fact that the Old Testament included personal enemies among the people to be loved, but excluded national enemies, who were equated with foes of God. Whatever qualifications of the principle may have been made, in later Judaism, by sensitive rabbis, the principle itself could hardly have been denied in the context of Jewish ethics. Contemporary Judaism itself draws the line of *non possumus* as soon as the welfare of the State of Israel seems, rightly or wrongly, to be threatened: there is no reconciliation with the national enemy.

As depicted in the New Testament, Jesus shows no awareness of this distinction. He neither alludes to national enemies nor remains indifferent to the Romans. He refers to no foes of God besides devils and demons. Likewise, one looks in vain in the Pauline Epistles for the suggestion that the followers of Jesus can have enemies. Whatever may have been the ethics of the Old Testament, the New Testament provides no evidence that

God has enemies among mankind. No national enmity can now be identified with the divine anathema.

In this case, who exactly is my neighbor according to the New Testament?[1]

♦ ♦ ♦ ♦ ♦

St. Luke's parable of the Good Samaritan (Luke 10:25–37) opens on a short dialogue between Jesus and a lawyer.[2] The lawyer asks a simple, honest question: "What must I do to inherit everlasting life?" This question is clearly about "the way," about proper behavior in the context of the Torah. Jesus replies with another question: "What is written in the Law? How do you read it?" The lawyer, a good Jew, conflates two major loci for the knowledge of "the way": words from the traditional prayer of Deuteronomy 6, the Shema' Israel, and words from Leviticus 19:18 about the commandments: "You shall love the Lord your God with all your heart, with all your soul, and with all your strength, and with all your mind; and your neighbor as yourself."

The lawyer pushes the enquiry further by asking: "And who is my neighbor?" This standard question of rabbinic reflection provides Jesus with an occasion to outline his understanding of love, through the maieutic or didactic form of a parable.

The solution is hidden in the tale of six men or six kinds of men: robbers, a Samaritan, a priest, a Levite, an innkeeper, an imprudent traveler. The listeners are invited to figure out the right answer. The puzzle relates to the relation of the first five persons to the sixth. Little need be said about the robbers, well-known characters in all societies. The priest and the Levite pass on, although, as professionally holy men, they would be expected to behave with compassion toward the victim. Since he is a heretic, publicly avoided by Jews, the Samaritan would not be expected to get involved with a Jew in need of help, for he might cause resentment even on the part of the person he could aid. The innkeeper is of course only a businessman who takes money for what he does.

As is proper to a good story, the unexpected happens. The victim is ignored by the priest and the Levite, and is assisted by the Samaritan. The heretic "was moved to pity at the sight." If we were to translate this more literally, we would have to say: he "was moved in his spleen."

Pity or compassion implies "suffering with." This is not physical pain. It is understanding of another's suffering through our common humanity. Compassion is not an intellectual, detached, objective judgment. It does not reside in the head. It is emotive, affective, and still located in the heart by popular imagination. The Hebrews placed it in the bowels, the liver, the spleen. Compassion is felt inside, in the guts. But compassion is not equated with love. The parable does not refer to *eros, philia,* or to what became the most common Christian word for love, *agape.* It evokes a feeling that is infinitely closer to the Buddhist concept of mercy or compassion.

In the context of the tale, the conclusion is formulated as a question: "Which of these three, in your opinion, was neighbor to the man who fell in with the robbers?" But the verb "to be," expressed here as "was," does not represent a permanent status, an ontic quality, a state. It results from an action. It is a coloration that one acquires, something that one becomes, a promotion to be deserved, a perfection to be obtained, a moral achievement. The lawyer understood this well, since he answered: "The one who treated him with compassion." The man who showed mercy, who was moved to compassion, became neighbor to the person he assisted. One becomes neighbor by experiencing empathy, by helping those in need, by having mercy on those who are in pain. Compassion initiates the dynamic relationship of neighborliness.

Not everyone is my neighbor, and I am not neighbor to everyone. My neighbor is the person who has compassion on me. The question is not: Who dealt with the victim as with a neighbor? It is: Who became neighbor to the victim? The neighbor is not the wounded traveler toward whom the Samaritan is moved to pity. Rather, the Samaritan makes himself neighbor to the victim. Unable to react, knocked out, the traveler is neighbor to no one. Of those who are in a position to act, only one makes himself neighbor to the victim. Thus the lesson is exactly the reverse of what is often assumed. It is commonly thought that the wounded man was the neighbor of all those who came on the scene but was so treated by the Samaritan alone. In reality, the lesson of the parable is quite different: no one becomes neighbor to another until he acts with compassion toward this other person.

But if no one is neighbor to another, all are invited to become neighbor to those who need them. Compassion and merciful action transform a stranger into a neighbor. Only at this point does love, *agape*, enter the picture. The person who has been shown compassion should love his neighbor as himself. Insofar as the Samaritan has become neighbor to the traveler, this man can now love him as his own self. Whether he does so the tale does not tell.

Love for the neighbor seems therefore to pass through two stages which are related dialectically. The first stage is compassion on the part of one person. The second is *agape* on the part of another who responds to the compassion of the first person. Having made myself neighbor to another, I can become the object and recipient of love-*agape*. If you wish to be loved, make yourself lovable. If you do not make yourself lovable, do not be surprised if no one loves you.

Compassion should be universal. I ought to show sympathy, affective understanding, for all, regardless of their status as citizens and of social conventions. This will make me neighbor to all. These in turn will have a chance to grow in *agape* toward me. I will be loved. *Agape* can be universal only to the extent that compassion is universal. I cannot love the person who feels no mercy on me. But I can have compassion on the person, become his or her neighbor and thus, hopefully, start that person on the road to love. Compassion refused can be the starting point of compassion offered—in the reverse order and by the other person to whom compassion has not been extended.

If all have compassion for one another, then *agape*, sparked in mutuality, becomes truly universal. Each sees the other as his neighbor since each has experienced merciful compassion from the other. Conversely, all become neighbor to all by feeling and showing empathy, sympathy, understanding, willingness, kindliness, friendliness. Thus, if the obligation to love one's neighbor leaves open the question, "Who is my neighbor?" the Gospel answer does not claim everyone as my neighbor. It suggests that I should recognize my neighbor at his compassionate attitude toward me. Such a person I can, and I ought to, love as my own self, because he has given himself to me in compassion.

◆ ◆ ◆ ◆ ◆

This perspective opens a reinterpretation of the Law as given in the Old Testament. The neighbor of the older revelation is a member of the chosen People or a friendly alien living in peace in the land of Israel. The neighbor of the New Testament need not belong to the Christian community. In the parable, he is even a heretic. Neighborliness is no longer tribal, national, institutional, traditional, social, conventional, racial. It is spiritual. The burden has been put on everyone to become neighbor to all so that all can love. The selectivity of *agape* will rest on a basis of universality, the full dimension of humanity being potentially included in compassion. The compassionate has become neighbor to all mankind. And why restrict compassion to humankind? Compassion can extend to the entire cosmos and its inhabitants.

This was the attitude of St. Isaac the Syrian:

> What is a charitable heart? It is a heart which is burning with charity for the whole of creation, for men, for birds, for beasts, for demons, for all creatures. He who has such a heart cannot see or call to mind a creature without his eyes becoming filled with tears by reason of the immense compassion which seizes his heart; a heart which is softened and can no longer bear to see or learn from others of any suffering, even the smallest pain, being inflicted upon a creature. This is why such a man never ceases to pray also for the animals, for the enemies of truth, and for those who do him evil, that they may be preserved and purified. He will pray even for reptiles, moved by the infinite pity which reigns in the heart of those who are becoming united to God.[3]

Under the name of charity, Isaac describes the compassion that makes *agape* possible. Such compassion extends to all creatures. It is significant that God is not included here among those who are reached by "charity." For God cannot be the object of mercy. God is infinite compassion, and for this reason all creatures are called to love God.

Such terms as charity, love, and their synonyms are often used ambiguously, as they can stand both for the compassion that is preliminary to the response of love, and for the love that responds to compassion. Yet the structure of Christian love begins clearly to emerge, despite the inadequacy of the vocabulary.

◆ ◆ ◆ ◆ ◆

But perhaps Luke 6:27–35 will suggest an objection to this analysis:

> To you who hear me, I say: Love your enemies, do good to those who hate you; bless those who curse you and pray for those who maltreat you. When someone slaps you on one cheek, turn and give him the other; when someone takes your coat, let him have your shirt as well. Give to all who beg from you. When a man takes what is yours, do not demand it back. Do to others what you would have them do to you. If you love those who love you, what credit is that to you? Even sinners love those who love them. If you do good to those who do good to you, how can you claim any credit? Sinners do as much. If you lend to those from whom you expect repayment, what merit is there in it for you? Even sinners lend to sinners, expecting to be repaid in full. Love your enemy and do good; lend without expecting repayment.

In this text, where the term *neighbor* does not appear, the verb *agapein* (to love) is applied both to the love that unites the disciples and to that which "sinners" show to one another. Luke's usual word for "mercy" is also missing. It is clear that *agapein* does not always carry the full connotation of Christian love. It is interchangeable with other verbs, such as *philein*. Likewise, the nouns, *agape, philia, eros,* are interchangeable, despite the fact that *agape* is characteristic of the Christian vocabulary. In other words, the term *agapein*, in Luke's Sermon on the Mount, does not necessarily identify love for the enemy with love for the neighbor. Love for the enemy can be no more than mercy on him. His being my enemy calls for compassion, forgiveness, reconciliation. Thus universal compassion reaches all, friends and foes alike, also those to whom I have been indifferent.

Luke 6 would then refer to the mercy that ought to become the ground for real love. By definition, the enemy is not a neighbor. Yet when I feel compassion for him, he is in a position to change enmity to love because I have made myself neighbor to him.

This universal scope of mercy is well emphasized in Matthew 5:45, where the compassionate person is likened to the Father in heaven who makes his sun to shine on the evil and the good. Luke also ends the quotation from his chapter 6 with the injunction: "Be compassionate, as your Father is compassionate."

The dialectic of mercy and love emerges explicitly now. By virtue of the mercy shown to an enemy, this enemy is faced with the occasion to love me as his own self because I have become neighbor to him. Only when he shows mercy or responds to mercy by love can I in turn love him as my neighbor. The central point of the Gospel teaching on love consists therefore in identifying the neighbor as the person who shows mercy. To love someone who feels no compassion is neither required nor even possible. Empathy is a prerequisite of love.

◆ ◆ ◆ ◆ ◆

Let us return to Unamuno and *The Tragic Sense of Life.* Is maternal love, identified as pity for the helpless child, the basic model of love? A mother does not love her baby as her neighbor, for the baby is not yet one. She identifies with this tiny, helpless human being who can do nothing in self-defense. Does a woman feel maternal love for a man when she gives herself to him to alleviate the sufferings of a creature who is helpless before a desire that he cannot fulfill without her? Is maternal love the type of Christian love? Male desire, aiming at conquest, is certainly not compassionate; yet it begs for mercy, for it can never fulfill itself. Thus it becomes an occasion of compassionate motherly love. Similar compassion can extend to all creatures and to the universe itself, which all suffer from the various forms of helplessness that belong to creatureliness. In this, Unamuno seems to have analyzed correctly the precondition for what I take to be love. But he has only given us a starting point. *Agape* goes further than compassion for suffering humankind.

It seems to me that the precondition of *agape* can be properly identified as justice. Compassion, mercy, empathy, sympathy, understanding, are subjective attitudes that strive for the founding of an order of justice in the world. Justice is the societal pattern in which one can truly say, with the father in the parable of the Prodigal Son: "Everything I have is yours" (Luke 15:31). Injustice denies mercy; it refuses assistance. The unjust person makes himself neighbor to no one, does not intend to become neighbor, does not wish to be loved. Injustice undermines *agape* from the start. Yet it can occasion mercy on the part of its victims. Mercy begins to correct injustice by positing the precondition of love.

Certain standards of justice are recognized in all societies. The twofold structure of love for neighbor demands that each one develop both an objective sense of justice and a subjective capacity to respond to injustice with mercy. For if a felt injustice makes love impossible, it makes compassion appropriate. One should have compassion on the unjust in order to forgive. Forgiveness makes us neighbor to them, even to those who do not remotely wish to be neighbor to us.

◆ ◆ ◆ ◆ ◆

The Christian attitude to others includes both compassion and *agape*. Where these are awake, the order of the Law is outmoded. The paradox of love is that a spiritual attitude becomes the focus of a New Law. But love is never a law; it is a principle of life. If the New Testament places love at the center of the Law, this can only be because the nature of law has changed radically. Law is no longer legalistic and literal; it is spiritual. It is created by love. If a Christian ought to love his neighbor as himself, this places on him the task of becoming neighbor to all in order to be loved by all and to live in a relationship of universal *agape*. How do I become neighbor to another? A stranger who walks along the street is not my neighbor. He does not know me and I have never met him. He has done nothing to be my neighbor. But if I establish a personal relationship to him through mercy, then I become his neighbor.

If all the disciples did this, universal love would prevail among them. All would be neighbor to all. All would respond to mercy with love.

Notes

1. There is an extensive bibliography on the New Testament doctrine on love. One can study the topic in exegetical and hermeneutical works, such as James Moffat, *Love in the New Testament* (New York: R. R. Smith, 1930); Ceslaus Spicq, *Agape in the New Testament*, 3 vols. (St. Louis: B. Herder, 1963, 1965, 1966), with bibliography, vol. 1, pp. 317–24. One can also study books of Christian ethics and their treat-

ment of the ethics of love in the New Testament, e.g., Paul Ramsay, *Basic Christian Ethics* (New York: Scribners, 1954).

2. It is clear that I am not trying to make an exhaustive exposition of love in the New Testament, or in the Synoptic Gospels, or even in St. Luke. Interested readers can be referred to the many commentaries on the New Testament and to Spicq's three volumes. The selection of Luke 10:25–37 for special reflection is justified by its importance in the New Testament: "One must recognize not only that the story of Luke 10:25–37 is homogeneous, but also that it constitutes one of the richest teachings of the Gospel on the love of charity" (Spicq, *Agape*, Vol. I, p. 141).

3. A. L. Wensinck, *Mystic Treatises of St. Isaac the Syrian* (Amsterdam: Koninklijke Akademie Van Wetenschapen, 1923), p. 341.

IV

Selective Love

In 1 Corinthians 12, St. Paul speaks of the many functions, charismata, gifts, and talents that are found in the Christian community, especially at Corinth and also, by analogy, in other churches.[1] The one Spirit of God inspires diverse functions for the many tasks to be performed in the organization of the Christian witness and worship. Some have wisdom, knowledge, faith, strength, prophecy, miracles, languages, interpretation of languages. All comes from and is done in the Spirit. The Spirit unites the disciples into one Body—the Body of Christ—in which distinctions and discriminations of this world are absorbed in love. There is neither Greek nor Jew, neither slave nor free man, neither male nor female. It would be futile to desire all the gifts for oneself and to be envious of the talents of others. The hand cannot envy the foot; but all the limbs work together for the oneness of the one body. There is room, in the Church, for apostles, prophets, teachers, for administrators, healers, speakers, translators.

Yet there are "greater gifts" (1 Cor. 12:31). These amount to one, the greatest, which 1 Cor. 13 describes as the charism of *agape*.

"Now I will show you the way which surpasses all the others." The perspective is also that of "the way." All truly ethical religion is a path. It teaches a certain type of behavior, an obedience to the Lord who expresses his will through the Torah and the prophets. This Jewish emphasis survives in the early Church with the theme of the "two ways," of life and of death (*Didache*), of light and of darkness (Epistle of Barnabas).[2] The way is of course a way of life. Philosophy, in the Greek world, and theology, in the nascent thinking of the Christian communities, are not speculative exercises, but practical disciplines pregnant with conclusions as to the better life. In this sense the Old Testament already identified belief with obedience rather than with distinct knowledge of certain truths. Likewise in the Greco-Roman context, philosophy is the love of wisdom; and wisdom is no abstract theory but a way of life expressed in personal commitment. Paul also presents *agape* as a way. Love will be more than feeling. It will involve both thought and action. There is no hint that love could be a romantic concept, an irrational urge, an uncontrollable force which would create its own rules regardless of either Law or Spirit. A way implies a philosophy and it therefore presupposes rationality.

The first section of chapter 13 states the supremacy of love: "If I have the gift of prophecy. . . if I have faith. . . but have not love, I am nothing." After verse 3, Paul lists the qualities of *agape*: "Love is patient; love is kind. Love is not jealous, it does not put on airs, it is not snobbish." With verse 8, love is projected into the future: "Love never fails." Smaller gifts will vanish, but love will remain through the future and for eternity. Of all the gifts from the Spirit, faith, hope and love persist through the eschatological transformations. But primacy belongs to love: "There are in the end three things that last: faith, hope and love, and the greatest of these is love."

This provides the link with chapter 14: "Seek eagerly

after love." Seek all the gifts of the Spirit if you wish, but seek *agape* most of all. In the sixteenth century, St. John of the Cross was to write: "On the last day, you shall be judged on love."[3]

◆ ◆ ◆ ◆ ◆

All other gifts are in some way exclusive. One cannot be at the same time apostle, prophet, teacher, administrator. But all can have love. *Agape* is offered to all by the Spirit.

Being a way, love does not remain static. Since it tends to unity with others, love inaugurates a development of interpersonal relationships. Love does not come to light in a vacuum, but its qualities emerge in relationships. It is in relation to concrete persons that love is patient, kind, unenvious. "There is no limit to love's forbearance, to its trust, its hope, its power to endure." In relation to others, there is nothing that love cannot face and absorb. Nothing lies beyond the trust, the hope, the endurance experienced in love. Love is the ground upon which trust, hope, endurance grow.

The way centered on *agape* demands a thorough acceptance of the otherness of others. Only in a framework of total respect, in full acknowledgment of the transcendence of others can we relate to human persons completely, in *agape*, becoming immanent to them and welcoming them into our own self. Not by confusion with the other can I become he or she. Yet a process of identification begins with the recognition and the acceptance of otherness. One never needs to identify with oneself, except in the lounges of psychiatrists. But love identifies me with the person I love. The movement of *agape* tends to promote the excellence, the privileges, the rights of others, opening the way to self-identification with this other, to self-transcendence by reaching into another.

Another characteristic of *agape* is mentioned at the end of the chapter: *agape* is the source of true knowledge. The passage to knowledge corresponds to the promotion from childhood to the adult age. "When I was a child I used to talk like a child, think like a child, reason like a child. When I became a man I put childish ways aside." In the present life, human creatures remain, in a sense, children; they are destined to grow into adulthood through a resurrection; they are to die and to rise with Christ into the fullness of humankind. Between "now" (*arti*) and "then" (*tote*), an eschatological transformation takes place. Love reaches fruition in the *parousia*, and this fruition implies true knowledge. There is an experiential, immediate presence of what is known. "Now we see indistinctly, as in a mirror; then we shall see face to face. My knowledge is imperfect now; then I shall know even as I am known." Love contains a kernel of knowledge which will be analogous to God's own knowledge. I shall know as I am known to the one who loves me. God loves me. I shall know as God already loves me. *Agape* inaugurates a higher rationality. You can really know only the person you love, the person who loves you. True knowledge is love.

Yet one may well ask: In St. Paul's perspective, is not such knowledge delayed till the resurrection? Is it reached only when we enter the Kingdom yet to come?

In reality, the two orders of childhood and adulthood, of partial knowledge and full knowledge, are already experienced in the two orders of the present life: "now" and "then" represent at this moment, within the context of the *ecclesia*, the pre-Christian way and the Christian way, the time before baptism and conversion and the time after initiation. "Now" symbolizes this earth, this body, this flesh, of which Paul exclaims: "Who can free me from this body under the power of death?" The moments before and after faith, which are dramatically described in the Epistle to the Romans, co-exist within the believer so that, what he does not wish to do, he does, what he wishes to do, he does not do. But if faith (*pistis*) cannot overcome the dichotomy between flesh and spirit, *agape* transcends it. The inner abyss of man is bridged. Now, today, I can know as I am known—if I have *agape*. In love I am no longer self-estranged by the struggle between flesh and spirit. I no longer hesitate in the realm of *psyche*, at the threshold of spirit. *Agape* introduces me to the true knowledge of myself and of the one I love.

In a time of partial knowledge, love anticipates full knowledge. When my time comes, I will know as I am known in God's love for me. My knowledge face to face with God will be somehow adequate, in mystery, to God's knowledge of me. Such knowledge by experience has been described many times by the mystics, with varying metaphors and in diverse perspectives. Theologians have tried to explain it. For the twelfth-century author William of St. Thierry, the experience of the love of God develops the similarity between man and God so that man, becoming more spiritual, acquires a knowledge of God's Spirit which intellectual research and reasoning could not provide.[4] Such a knowledge, St. Thomas Aquinas carefully points out, is not "connatural" but "super-natural": it is not the natural powers of the human mind that bring it about, but the undeserved grace of God which strengthens the will and the intellect of man so that they can receive it.[5] Following St. Augustine, both Thomas Aquinas and St. Bonaventure distinguished between "morning knowledge" and "afternoon knowledge." Before the creation of the cosmos, angels could know future realities by contemplating God's foreknowledge: knowing God, they knew in him all there was to know. After the material creation, angels know things and events as these are in their concrete reality; through things and events, they acquire a second knowledge of God as reflected in his works. But with us, human persons, the order is reversed. We start from afternoon knowledge (knowing God through his works), and we walk in pilgrimage toward morning knowledge (knowing God in himself, and his works in him). The former is acknowledgment; the latter is full knowing by way of love. Love is the link and the bridge between "now" and "then," between sunset and sunrise.[6]

We have thus passed, perhaps without realizing it, from love for human persons to love for God. St. Paul starts his chapter 13 with the first and ends it with the second. But is there a real difference between the two loves? Is not the structure of *agape* one? Is there not one structure only for all love, whether it is called *agape*, or *philia*, or *eros*?

◆ ◆ ◆ ◆ ◆

Before attempting to answer these questions, I would like to examine how, if at all, St. Paul's encomium of love fits my understanding of the parable of the Good Samaritan. If indeed the total movement of love for the neighbor undergoes the two stages of mercy and of *agape*, to which one does Paul refer?

Clearly, Paul does not allude to the mercy which makes a person neighbor to another. This is only a precondition; it is not the fulfillment of *agape*. Yet Paul's description does not tally with the second phase of the process of universal love, with the response to mercy in loving the merciful neighbor. The *agape* of 1 Corinthians 13 reaches further than Luke's love for the neighbor. It is deeper. It is warmer. Possibly, Paul is not thinking of phases in the process of love, but of the totality, and thus encompassing mercy and response at one glance. Yet there remains the possibility that Paul is actually referring to something else.

This is precisely, at this point, my hypothesis: the New Testament describes, not only the two types of love that contribute to the formation of the Christian *agape*, but also a higher form of this *agape*.

Universal mercy reaches everyone in need, be this a friend, a casual acquaintance, a stranger, an enemy. Popular parlance calls this "love" or "love for the neighbor." Yet it would be better to speak of mercy or compassion. It makes love for the neighbor possible by creating neighborliness. My compassion makes me neighbor to others and worthy of a neighbor's love.

Love for the neighbor, identified with the second commandment of the Law—which is equal to the first—is the response of a person to the one who has become neighbor through compassion. One cannot love an enemy like a neighbor since, by definition, an enemy does not exhibit the compassion that would make him our neighbor. But toward enemies one may feel compassion. Love for the neighbor goes to those who cannot be enemies because they have made themselves our neighbors. This second step, stage, phase, or degree of Christian love may or may not last, for the circumstances in which compassion is expressed and remembered may be altered radically. Having been helped in temporary circumstances of dire need, I may be extremely grateful and love my neighbor deeply. Yet the relationship that has been established may never be resumed because I may never meet this person again. This suggests that such a love for the neighbor can also occasion a more lasting, deeper relationship: it can lead to another step, stage, phase, degree, kind, or type of love.

It is this further sort of *agape* which, as I understand it, Paul describes. This is the perfection of love, the fruition of the total gift of self. It implies something that does not yet occur in compassion or in gratitude. This love and gift is described by Paul at its peak, in relation to God. But it also develops within human relationships. It may be called friendship. God and his creatures become friends. Man and man, woman and woman, man and woman, become friends. Friendship constitutes the ultimate form of *agape*, the perfection of Christian love. In relation to God, *agape* means God-with-us, Emmanuel, the gift of God in his Son born, crucified, and risen for us. Already God's creation shines with God's mercy. But his friendship with man, his "philanthropy," is something else. It is that which mystics of all religions have experienced and witnessed to. It is that of which we catch a glimpse when we truly love God.

Among human relationships, the fullness of *agape* is neither mercy nor gratitude. It is the sharing of friendship. If compassion is or at least ought to be universal, being ready to help anyone in need in any circumstances foreseeable and unforeseeable, if love for the neighbor is potentially universal, being returned in gratitude to all who are neighbor to us, friendship cannot be universal. It is necessarily selective.

◆ ◆ ◆ ◆ ◆

Like the synoptic Gospels, the Gospel of John is entirely focused on the sacrifice of love made by Jesus.[7] A special note is added in that Jesus is identified as the *Logos* made flesh, the One in whom Life is, the true Light which illumines every human person. Those who meet him, such as John the Baptist (1:29–51), Mary at Cana (2:1–12), Nicodemus (3:1–21), the woman in Samaria (4:1–42), the officer at Capernaum (4:43–53), the paralytic (5:1–9), the man born blind (9:1–41), Martha and Mary (11:17–44); and also the Judaeans (*passim*), the crowd, which I take to mean the "people of the soil" (*lam ha 'eretz*), the poor peasants (6:22–40); and especially the disciples, are face to face with God's love fully manifested in a man. The conclusion of the Gospel is adequately formulated in the question addressed to Simon: "Do you love me?" (21:15–17). This is the question implicitly but unmistakably addressed by Jesus, the Son of God, to all who encounter him.

In his first Epistle,[8] John sums up his theology in the confession, which is both a doxology and a principle of behavior: "Beloved, let us love one another, because love is of God; everyone who loves is begotten of God and has knowledge of God. The man without love has known nothing of God, for God is love" (1 John 4:7–8). God is no abstract love. He is the very concrete Love sending the only Son into the world. "Love, then, consists in this: not that we have loved God, but that he has loved us and has sent his Son as an offering for our sins" (4:10).

Christian love is the experience of God's love as it is manifested in sharing what we are with others. "One who has no love for the brother he has seen cannot love the God he has not seen" (4:21).

◆ ◆ ◆ ◆ ◆

The disciples are expected to love all human persons. This traditional understanding of the ethics of the Gospel constitutes the basic stance of the Christian faith in the area of human relationships. But, in keeping with the foregoing analysis, this can only mean that the disciples should have compassion for all, that they should be totally open to the upsurge of mercy for the misery of the universe and the universal anguish of human beings. By the same token, the disciples are called to respond to all expressions of compassion with thanksgiving and gratitude. But friendship cannot be an obligation. It is not a law. It is grace. The acme of *agape* requires selectivity. It can take place only among a small number of persons. It demands the sort of depth in exchange which is possible only among the few.

The objection may be raised that this would make Christian love discriminatory. But is this really an objection? Were enemy and friend to be treated in the same way on the basis of their common humanity, the one in spite of being an enemy, the other in spite of being a friend, what would friendship mean? Such a love would be radically detached from human relationships. Friendship does make a difference to behavior. Hatred and enmity present tremendous obstacles to overcome for civilized behavior. Unacquaintance makes people shy away from one another. The object of Christian love is not mankind in general, since mankind never appears to anyone in daily experience. Only concrete men and women exist. Only concrete persons enter our life. We cannot experience friendship with the Eskimo we have never met and we are not likely to meet. Admittedly, if love cannot unite me to an unknown person, I can still be disposed to love that person when I perceive that he or she is my neighbor. Eventually we can also acquire friendship. As I understand it, the Christian concept of universal love implies the first two attitudes, mercy and the response it evokes, compassion and love for the neighbor. It does not extend to the level of friendship, which is necessarily selective.

◆ ◆ ◆ ◆ ◆

The lesson to be drawn may seem disconcerting. For we end up with a paradox. The Christian injunction to love applies first to compassion, then to the grateful response to the compassionate, which constitutes love for the neighbor. Can we add that the Gospel invitation to love includes, in a certain way, friendship?

Christian love has always been understood, not as a legal obligation, but as a movement by which persons never rest satisfied with any given expression of love, but always seek further to give themselves more thoroughly. Love is a direction. It tends to an ideal which may never be reached. In this precisely the paradox of the New Testament lies. Friendship is selective. Yet it is the ideal around which all disciples should be united. In other words, Christian love must have three levels rather than two. At each level the universality of love is maintained. Yet it is not implemented in the same way at all levels. And it may well be that it cannot be implemented at all at the third level. Friendship also ought to be universal; yet this cannot possibly be realized in the conditions of the present life.

This point may be illustrated with the dialectic of the one and the many. In the Bible, the many are frequently represented by the few. The People of God is represented by prophets who speak to it and for it, by saints, by kings, by priests, by a "small remnant" of holy people, by the Servant of Yahweh. Yet this does not change the covenant with the whole People, since, in the eyes of God, the few stand for the many. In the New Testament, the many have been multiplied to the point of encompassing the whole of mankind. Reversely, the few have dwindled to the one man Jesus Christ. Yet the covenant is kept alive and renewed, for, in the eyes of God, Jesus gives himself for all human beings.

Such a perspective gives a deeper connotation to several biblical passages on love.

"I give you a new commandment: love one another. Such as my love has been for you, so must your love be

for each other. This is how all will know you for my
disciples: your love for one another" (John 13:34–35).
This expresses, not the obligation of universal mercy and
of love for the neighbor, but the invitation to friendship.
In the context, friendship is possible among the disciples
because there are few of them.

"Again I tell you, if two of you join your voices on
earth to pray for anything whatever, it shall be granted
you by my Father in heaven. Where two or three are
gathered in my name, there am I in their midst" (Matt.
18:19–20). Jesus is not with the crowd. He is with the
two's and three's. For only with two or three is friendship possible. The love that coincides with the presence
of Christ is that of two or three, as experienced in friendship. In the context of friendship, the small group stands
for the whole Church. It is symbolically, mystically,
identical with the Church and it expresses the whole
purpose of God in relation to humankind. It anticipates
the joy of the Kingdom. The multitude is brought down
to the small remnant, to the community of friends. The
two or three represent the many in messianic mediation.
Christianly speaking, I can love all human persons only
to the extent that I have found the one or two with whom
I identify in friendship. The *agape* described by Paul, the
Christian ideal of love, is friendship. It can exist in this
life only in relation to the few because of the psychological, sociological, and spiritual impossibility of total
communion with the many. I should seek for the one or
two, the friends, with whom I can experience total love,
and without whom I cannot love anyone in a Christian
way. For the many I can feel compassion. To the compassion of many I can respond with love for the neighbor.
But *agape*, in its fullness, reaches the point of identification with concrete persons. These are loved concretely as

they are. And they also represent the *ecclesia*, the assembly of the children of God through whom God sees and projects all humankind. You have with the chosen few the relationships you would like to have, but cannot possibly have, with the common many.

In such a perspective, *agape*, though selective, need not be exclusive. A latent universal dimension opens it to the possible inclusion of others in the intimate bonds of friendship. Friendship is never closed, even when the maximum number of persons possible for optimum friendship has been reached. This number may vary with the loving capacities of each. Yet friendship always remains open to the further possibilities of new circumstances and events. Love is always, at this level also, a movement, a direction. The search for friendship never ceases, for the capacity to love is never exhausted. Love is never a commodity, it is always an exigency.

Friendship, *agape* in the full sense of the term, unites human persons who identify with each other despite and within their otherness. But the widest otherness and the closest identity are experienced between a man and a woman. Thus the man-woman relationship forms the central model of the Christian *agape* as mutual self-gift. As *agape*, love between a man and a woman is a way of spiritual life, a search for spiritual fulfillment, a growth toward spiritual perfection, a sacrament of the Lord's presence with two or three. It is open and inclusive, though radically selective. Such a love need not imply sexual relationship, although sexual congress may adequately express and fulfill an identity in otherness which has already been achieved psychologically and spiritually. Nor should one confuse with agapic love a sexual relationship prompted by self-love and focused on physical pleasure. This makes real love impossible. For it tends to taking and appropriating the other, whereas *agape,* in its sexual expression also, moves two persons to give themselves totally to each other.

One may well wonder about the implications of this perspective for the institution and the experience of Christian marriage. The basic consequence is obvious: marriage ought first of all to be friendship. *Agape* should be a precondition for marriage. A man and a woman who are not even friends in the total spiritual sense of the word attempt marriage at their own risk. They are likely to run headlong into the breakdown of their relationship under the clash of two egoisms. Yet, in the structure of *agape,* marital love adds to friendship only a stable way of life that makes the frequent sexual expression of love possible. It adds a context of life-long living together and a covenant of sexual sharing. The qualities of marriage-love are exactly those of friendship-love: selectivity, openness, representativeness, fidelity. The demands may be more strenuous since living together is a school of abnegation. But marriage neither exhausts nor cancels the need and the duty of friendship. The circle of friendship always remains virtually broader than that of marriage, or else the two will mistake their representativeness for exclusiveness. Selfishness for two is the opposite of *agape,* and it ruins equally marriage and friendship.

◆ ◆ ◆ ◆ ◆

This chapter is entitled "Selective Love." Love is indeed selective in its highest and most intimate forms. Yet its scope remains universal. If the Lord dwells with the two or three gathered together in his Name, then the universe also is with them. To be gathered in his Name means to be together in *ecclesia,* aware of the place and function of *agape* in the horizon of faith. *Agape* is selective in the persons it binds together intimately. Yet it is open to all. It is symbolically universal because in the eyes of God the few stand for the many and intercede for the many.

Notes

1. Most of Spicq's Vol. 2 (*Agape in the New Testament*) is dedicated to St. Paul; the Pastoral Epistles, which are, in Spicq's judgment, authentic, are treated at the beginning of Vol. 3. Again, I am not trying to write a full treatment of the Pauline doctrine on love. On Paul's teaching in 1 Corinthians, see T. G. Bunch, *Love: A Comprehensive Exposition of 1 Cor. XIII* (Washington: Review and Herald, 1952).

2. Robert Kraft, *Barnabas and the Didache*, The Apostolic Fathers series, ed. Robert Grant, 6 vols. (New York: Nelson, 1965), Vol. 3, pp. 137–62.

3. St. John of the Cross, "Dichos de Luz y Amor," n. 57, in *Vida y Obras de San Juan de la Cruz*, ed. Crisogono de Jesus, Biblioteca de Auctores Christianos (Madrid: Editorial Catolica, 1950), p. 57.

4. William of St. Thierry, *Exposition on the Song of Songs*, n. 1, trans. Columba Hart, in *The Works of William Thierry*, ed. M. Basil Pennington, Cistercian Fathers series, Vol. 6 (Kalamazoo, Mich.: Cistercian Publications, 1970), pp. 3–4.

5. Thomas Aquinas, *Summa theologica*, I, q. 13, aa. 2–5.

6. Augustine, *De Genesi ad litteram*, bk. 4, ch. 22 (PL 34:312); Bonaventure, *On the Sentences*, II, dist. iv, a. 3; Thomas Aquinas, *Summa theologica*, III, q. 9, a. 3. See Tavard, "St. Bonaventure as Mystic and Theologian" in Margaret Schatkin, ed., *The Heritage of the Early Church* (Rome: Oriental Institute, 1973), pp. 289–306.

7. On the doctrine of love in the Johannine writings, see Spicq, *Agape*, Vol. 3; C. H. Dodd, *The Interpretation of the Fourth Gospel* (Cambridge: Cambridge University Press, 1953); Edwin K. Lee, *The Religious Thought of St. John* (London: Allenson, 1950).

8. See below, Chapter 6.

V

The Structure of Love

The question of the structure of love refers to two related problems.[1] First, most analysts distinguish between many forms of love. The word *love* becomes equivocal, covering different emotions and attitudes that have little in common. The range is wide, from the desire to acquire an object to the totally self-abandoned love of God. By and large this has been the standard interpretation of love in Christian reflection. Is love one or many? Is there only a Hindu or Buddhist type of universal compassion, which takes many forms in human relationships? Should we endorse C. S. Lewis's classification of "four loves," or the more classical scholastic distinction of three loves, *concupiscentia, benevolentia, amicitia,* or Martin D'Arcy's explanation that there are two kinds of love, corresponding to *animus* and *anima?* Should we follow or borrow the insights of the Oriental tradition, whose quintessence is embodied in Zen: there is no radical difference between the union of the soul with God in mysticism, the attraction of man and woman for each other, the complementarity of the wind and the wave?

Second, a basic option between two approaches ought to be made. Classical Western definitions have called love several phenomena of mutual attraction. Love is seen as a desire, a nisus, a direction, a movement. Religiously speaking, it calls for conversion, turning oneself, changing one's orientation, discovering one's sun or, in St. Augustine's language, one's weight.[2] It seeks to awaken a similar desire and orientation in the other person, for whom I yearn, whom my love expects also to move and to convert. Love manifests a profound dynamism. It is never static. Peace and quiet, when they are obtained, fulfillment, when it is reached, prepare further desires, further movements, further actions, further conversions. It passes from dynamism to dynamism. To it one can apply the expression of the Gospel of John: "Of his fullness we have all had a share—love following upon love" (John 1:16). We can also discern in it the pattern of the Jewish and the Christian revelation, which goes from promise to fulfillment, the fulfillment containing the germs of a higher promise leading to a higher fulfillment.[3] Yet classical definitions also include in love an element of communion, of attainment, of fulfillment, of harvesting, of fruition. At its acme, love brings satisfaction, tranquillity, quiet, peace. It no longer seeks because it has found. It need not progress because it has been made perfect. But if this is indeed so, then love must include both desire and fulfillment. Then the question arises: Is love the desire or the fulfillment? Which of these two predominates in the structure of love?

Here again, Christian reflection has more usually adopted the standpoint of motion. Love is a desire, a drive, determined by its object or project. Diverse forms of love follow from the diversity of what we desire. If love is desire, then it must be manifold since many objects, things, persons, are desirable, and some seem to be at times supremely to be desired. But if love is fulfillment, then diversity applies only to the steps toward it: intermediate goals lead to the highest goal. Even at lower rungs of the ladder of love, love aims ultimately at the highest point, the final goal, beyond which there is no further desire and no further fulfillment.

◆ ◆ ◆ ◆ ◆

I propose to answer the second question first. Granted that love implies desire and tends to a concrete object, it is the object—be it one or many—that will determine whether love is one or plural. Should we posit the alternative, we would have to postulate that love is not specified by an object and that the multiplicity of objects and of loves vanish. Precisely, I would define love as a structure—that is, as an ordering, a self-contained and self-explanatory phenomenon of order, a unity of more than one term defined by the condition of their oneness and not by the terms themselves. It is one, regardless of what realities may be united in love.

Such an approach seems to correspond to human experience. If we gather the elements that are common to what is usually called love, we obtain something like the following gradation:

1. I like something or someone: an object attracts me.

2. I desire something or someone: I orient myself in the direction of what attracts me.

3. I love someone, wishing to be with this person, enjoying a presence, feeling a want and an absence.

4. I love someone, trying to please this person, placing myself at his or her service.

5. I love someone, as a friend who has become part of my life.

6. I love someone, as mutual attraction and correlative responses lead us to share our lives.

One element underlies all such experiences and whatever intermediate steps one could discover or imagine between them: there is unity, at varying degrees and with many forms, between beings. At all levels, oneness emerges at the very point where love is acknowledged. Before I love someone, I feel an anticipation that is analogous to precomprehension in the experience of knowledge. Anticipation leads to the oneness without which there is no love. Love is thus structured around the polarities of unity and diversity. It is a communion between beings (persons) by which these are one within their very distinctiveness.

Such a structure provides a sufficient definition of love, which removes the necessity of paying attention to the persons themselves that are joined in love, and of analyzing the type of oneness in which they are joined. But it follows that love exists wherever one may detect unity among diverse realities. Love is manifested at all levels where creatures are capable of union, from mineral or vegetal beings to highly spiritual persons. Spiritual love unites minds or spirits. Corporeal love unites things or bodies. Human persons partake of both, and so does their love. Human love is inseparably *agape* and *eros*, self-gift and other-desire.

Since it is a matter of form rather than content, of structure rather than subject, love may be seen at all levels of being and existence. It is, in this sense, a universal phenomenon. But this can be true only if God—who is not within being yet who imprints his image upon all beings—is also love. Love in the created world implies an imitation of, a participation in, the reality of God as love.

◆ ◆ ◆ ◆ ◆

The first Epistle of John does not explain the inner meaning and the implications of its statement: "God is love." To some extent it draws out the human consequences of divine love. If God is love, man also should be love. The structure of oneness and distinction has marked creation. The universal attraction of masses is a material form of love. Human persons experience love. Love is found analogically in all reality.

Medieval thinkers accepted Aristotle's principle that "being and goodness converge upon oneness" (*Ens et bonum ad unum convertuntur*). *Ens* is the concrete existent being. *Bonum* is the good, or the aspect of each reality which attracts and inspires love, the loving capacity of every creature. All tends to unity with the good it perceives in others. Thus everything that has being also has openness to love. If something is, it is one and it loves. It shares the pattern of distinction and unity. It is never alone but is directed toward the other outside of itself.

Accordingly it is not surprising that all religions have placed some form of love at the center of their concerns. Whatever the differences between Buddhist compassion and Christian *caritas*, these share a common structure which impels human persons to unity with others. Each is sensitive to some aspect of the good which is a quality of all being.

Yet the Johannine conception goes further. By equating God with love, it adumbrates the idea of God as Trinity. If God is love, divine Being can be expressed in terms of the structure of love. Love being a communion between terms which remain distinct, distinction and oneness will be found in God. Classical theology speaks of unity of nature and distinction of persons. Unity is a basic ground which differentiates itself into a triad in such a way that each of the three terms enfolds in itself the fullness of the basic ground. In this line, Richard of St. Victor understood the Trinity as the immanent unfolding of God as love:[4] God is one love; yet this one love is the lover's love (the Father), the beloved's love (the Son), their mutual correlation as one shared love (the Spirit).

To say that God is love is also to say that, as his Being is
the ground of all being, divine love underlies and is
immanent to all that is. It overflows into creation and is
the reason for God's creative action. God communicates
himself to those he creates. Creation is the very act of the
divine self-communication to what is not God. Creation
is thus, in its core, a relationship of love between God
·and the universe, a oneness between the Creator and the
creature. Although all things are made in their individuality, they are not autonomous but theonomous. God is
all in all. His relationship to his creature is analogous to
the inner relationship by which God is one and three.
Divine love sustains the world in being. This being is
itself love. Creaturely being implies union with God, on
the part of those whom God makes distinct from himself.
The oneness in distinction of the One and the many is the
ground of all that is.

In the Christian view, love also takes the form of the
incarnation of God.[5] The divine Beloved becomes man.
He enters the realm of God's created love. He is now
loved as one of creation. Reversely, being united to the
Word made flesh, human persons enter the realm of
God's immanent love. To be one with Christ means to
share the divine filiation and to receive the Father's love.
Through the incarnation, human persons participate in
the life of the divine Beloved. Classical theology calls this
an "appropriation." Granted that the divine nature differentiates itself into threeness in keeping with the
threefold structure of love, it maintains that God always
acts, in relation to the universe, by virtue of his oneness.
Together, as one, the Father, the Son, the Spirit unite
creation to themselves. However, when we try to envis-
age the divine persons in the actions of the divine nature,
we tend to attribute to the divine persons, by way of
symbolization, aspects of our own reflection. Thus the

Father is called Creator, the Son Redeemer, the Spirit Sanctifier.

It seems to me, nevertheless, that the structure of love invites us to follow another line. If creation is an act of divine love, then the creatures do participate in the divine Beloved and they are recipients of the Father's love. The redemption effected by the Incarnate Lord establishes a unique relationship between the creatures and himself. Sanctification implies the experience of the Spirit in the Christian life: each human person is uniquely related to the Spirit, in a relationship that is necessarily univocal.

◆ ◆ ◆ ◆ ◆

In the structure of love, distinction is the starting point, the datum of nature. Unity is the end point, the construction of culture.

The origin is shrouded in a mystery of self-identity: Why is each person himself and not another self? Why am I I rather than he or she? The mystery of my self-identity is at the root of my search for unity with another who I am not, but who I could have been. The puzzle of why I am not another sparks my basic desire for unity with the one I could have been. There is thus a spontaneous wish for unity with others. It is of course entirely possible to stifle this drive for unity, to extinguish any wish to love and be loved. The drive to love dies easily, from selfishness. But if the fundamental wish to love can be killed, it can also be nurtured. Love normally seeks the person with whom union is possible and the level of union which is concretely attainable. The total oneness of human beings includes several levels. It requires a total sharing of souls and it may be expressed in a total sexual gift. But such a degree of sharing is not possible with just anyone. Love chooses. There may be degrees of spontaneity in this choice. It may grow slowly, as we realize our dissatisfaction with our own self-centeredness and our need and capacity for companionship. It may come rapidly through a sudden plunge into one's depths.

In any case, love entails liberation from self. Unity with another requires going out of self in order to give myself. It therefore implies the freedom to go. But if there are degrees of spontaneity, there are also degrees of freedom and degrees of awareness of love. Yet if it is not everyone who is aware of seeking oneness with others, the main point is the search rather than the awareness. If the word "I" symbolizes the self that I am, this "I" seeks for the "We" of a community in which I share the self of others.[6]

The motivation of love is to seek "We." The means—not always consciously understood although it derives from the deepest urge of a human person—is to give one's own self to others in an interpersonal relationship of total gift. Interpersonal exchange creates a bond that transforms the personalities of those involved in it. We cannot remain the same as when we were self-centered. The "I" becomes the "I" of a "We." In this movement love is profoundly and radically creative. The unrestricted giving of self between two persons in complete reciprocity creates a new world characterized by the sharing of the deepest levels of personhood. This world never existed before, because such a relationship is ever new.

At this point, unity in distinction becomes personal unity in personal distinction. It is not a matter of juxtaposition, of an accidental coincidence of opposites. Such a oneness is spiritual. The expression of interpersonal unity belongs to the spiritual level, even when it is mediated through the human body and human sexual-

ity. Without this spiritual dimension there is no true
love. The spiritual dimension of interpersonal love is
commensurate with its creativity: it creates a new world
of spiritual relationships.

> Only love can transform calculating justice into creative
> justice. Love makes justice just. Justice without love is
> always injustice because it does not do justice to the other
> one nor to myself nor to the situation in which we meet. So
> the other one, and I, and we together in this moment in
> this place are a unique and unrepeatable occasion calling
> for a unique and unrepeatable act of uniting love. If this
> call is not heard by listening love, if it is not obeyed by the
> creative genius of love, injustice is done. And this is true
> even of oneself. He who loves listens to the call of his own
> innermost center, and obeys this call, and does justice to
> his own being.[7]

In this passage Paul Tillich formulates the point I wish to
emphasize. Each time we meet another person we are in
a situation where a new world of spiritual relationships
becomes possible. Then everything lies open to the
creativity of love. As already noticed by the Socrates of
Plato's *Banquet,* love is creative.[8] It creates the only thing
that human persons can create, spiritual relationships.
Transforming matter through technology, we create
nothing. But when total love unites a man and a woman
in full spiritual unity, a new world is created. An event
takes place that was not there before. Persons enter
together into a new relationship. This is the highest type
of artistry because it takes place at the level of spirit, and
it is also the most concrete because it can be expressed
bodily. The wish to create is a basic human desire which
impels people to work. It is also the root of love. By
creating this new world, human persons are fulfilled as
images of God. And since the act of creation as such is
the prerogative of God, those who enter an unrestricted

relationship with others fulfill their possibilities as persons made in the likeness of the Creator.

It is basic to the ideas I am unfolding that love remains one in the many forms it may take. The oneness of love may be perceived in the means by which the new creation takes place. Essentially what this means is the gift of self to another in mutuality. I enter this new world by giving my being. We create something new insofar as we give ourself to another person capable of receiving us with attention, insight, and understanding. We offer ourselves like an open book to read. Our interior world is uncovered and discovered. At the same time we also discover the interior world of the person we love. Our self-gift is the starting point of a mutual journey into the depths of each other. Meeting and finding each other, entering each other's interior universe is not an ordinary tourist's travel. What is there to see in the interior world of another person? Simply, what nature and culture have placed and developed there. The richer our interior world, the more we can give and the more fully we can be loved. People with empty lives have nothing to give. Persons with deep spiritual, artistic, intellectual, emotional lives have much to offer to another person's loving scrutiny.

The more we love, the better we understand the universe of another person. For we understand a universe only by entering it. The more facets to our inner experience, the more relationships we can establish. "Whoever has will be given more" (Luke 19:26). Great saints are capable of great loves. They have much to give and great capacity to receive. In order to love, one must be attentive to the other, and receptive of his or her gift. Thus what is given in love is never lost, for it is always shared. One giving means two sharing.

There is no full sharing without reciprocity. Is it possi-

ble to love without being loved in return? Is love necessarily mutual or can it be one-sided? I personally do not
think it can be totally one-sided. Nothing is shared unless more than one person are involved in the sharing.
One cannot love fully without experiencing reciprocity,
without eliciting a response. Yet there are degrees of love
that are not always returned.

A new element should be introduced in the structure
of love at this point. Unity in distinction implies that "I"
seeks to become "We." Let me now suggest that this is
because, at a level that still lies below the normal level of
consciousness, "I" already shares in "We." One could
speak of two levels of the self, the conscious I-level and
the subconscious We-level. Or one could say that each
person has two selves, that of its own-centeredness and
that of its other-centeredness. The self is both individual
and collective while being personal throughout. Being
distinct, it enables a person to feel and to say "I." Yet it is
also the "We" of mankind. If creation is made out of
divine love, then it implies unity in distinction, one
"We" encompassing many "I's." If this is correct, then
even unreturned love implies participation in a "We"
which encompasses my "I" and the "I" of the other
whom I try to love and who does not seem to love me.

Such a conception does not destroy the freedom of
love. If all is love, if all human persons love without
sometimes realizing it, one might object that the experience of love is a banality. Yet awareness makes all the
difference. Facing God, human creatures are in a situation of unawareness. God is never loved to the fullest
extent possible and desirable. God gives himself without
expecting to be properly welcome. He does not entertain
the hope that someone some day will love him fully and
give him all glory. Yet God's love for mankind is fulfilled
because love is always satisfied with the answer that the

other has the capacity to give. Should I love a woman, I cannot tell her to what degree she should love me, but I am happy at what she has the capacity to give me. I do not make myself the standard of the love I receive. If someone has no capacity for self-giving, I can still be satisfied, or at least reconciled, with not being fully loved in return. Ideal love is fully shared and entirely mutual. It is a new world created by persons who establish a community together. Personal life creates common life. On this ground Christianity has traditionally stressed the organic relationships of the disciples, the corporateness of the Church, the liturgy as common worship transcending the private piety of each. Here also love creates a new sharing experience. When the Acts of the Apostles depicted the early believers as forming a community, Luke was aware of the creative power of the new faith. Whoever is united to Christ is united thereby to all those in whom Christ is present. The mystical body is erected on the foundation of creation. The love that has been transformed by salvation is grounded in the "We" in which all "I's" are one in humankind.

That the self is fundamentally twofold in the experience of love does not belittle the notion of individuality or personality. Rather, the individual personality of a human being hides a deeper personality which can only speak as "We" and which ultimately belongs to all mankind. This collective personality surfaces in the experience of love. The fuller our love, the more universal our awareness of this collective personality. If indeed the experience of love between a man and a woman can be the deepest and can imply the most complete gift of self, this is because each fulfills the role of mankind in relation to the other. In the perspective of Christian faith, each embodies the Christ for the other. Yet, if the one can stand for the many, one never replaces the many. For this reason a selfish love is self-destroying. Love shrinks and withers under the weight of selfishness. A love that is open to others and radiates around grows in generosity. It is more completely fulfilled and fulfilling.

If indeed love reveals that we participate in a collective personality which belongs to mankind, then can love ever die? Love initiates men and women to new relationships. Since it corresponds to the deeper layers of life, it ought to abide for ever. Yet men and women have also made the experience of the death of love, of the breaking of friendship, of the wrecking of marriage, through self-withdrawal, through mutual loathing, through indifference, through the search for sexual adventure. Behind such catastrophes there looms the simple principle and requirement that love cannot progress without justice, and if love does not grow, it dies. Love achieves oneness; justice maintains distinction. As unity in distinction, love must never be without the dimension of justice. Justice respects the distinction between those who love one another. Love thrives within this distinction. It tends to shrink when the distinction is blurred. Unity may have been foreseen. But if the distinctiveness of those who were uniting has not been respected, then love has been stifled by lack of justice. Injustice kills love. Disrespect for the other, for his or her "I," destroys the possibility of unreserved commitment. Whatever the ontological substratum of love, it is impossible to give my own self to one I do not respect or who does not respect me. Love dies when I discover that the other does not respect the source of love in me. The order of justice has not been preserved. Love dies when the commitment to unity is not kept. Unity may then have been sought on a narrow or partial basis. But love is total or it is not.

◆ ◆ ◆ ◆ ◆

This line of thought suggests no less than a convergence of the Western sense of the "I," of the self in its individuality, with the Eastern sense of the voiding of all selves in a discovery of the whole.[9] The "I" voids itself to the extent that it is open to the "We" of others, which is ultimately the "We," not only of mankind but of the universe. The spiritual traditions of Africa can teach us insights into the conditions, components, and exigencies of this cosmic "We" that will help bridge the gap between the "I" of Western thought and experience and the "non-I" of Eastern thought and experience.[10] These insights will be found to be anticipations and preparations of the Christian belief that, in the mystical body of Christ, in the communion of saints, in the *ecclesia*, all the faithful are one, members of one another and sharers in the same divine life. The belief in the incarnation and the experience of its grace through the sacramental life are not alien to the basic structure and to the intimate purpose of humankind at the level of creation: they deepen and sometimes reveal a dimension of all life, the dimension of love, the dimension of the "We."

Notes

1. This question has been studied many times, and there are as many solutions as there are authors. Besides the previously cited books by Nygren, D'Arcy, Williams, and Toner, see C. S. Lewis, *The Four Loves* (New York: Harcourt, Brace, 1971). I am in more congenial agreement with those who, like Harper and Toner, see love as fundamentally one, than with the authors who divide love into heterogeneous forms or structures.

2. *Amor meus pondus meus* (Augustine, *Confessions*, xiii, ix, 10 in *Oeuvres de saint Augustin* [Paris: Aubier, 1962], Vol. 14, p. 441). On the Augustinian concept of love, see ditto, "Notes complementaires," n. 23, pp. 617–22.

3. On the promise-fulfillment pattern of Christian life and truth, see Dietrich Ritschl, *Memory and Hope* (New York: Macmillan, 1968).

4. Richard of St. Victor, *De Trinitate*, bk. 3, ch. 19, Sources chrétiennes, n. 63 (Paris: Le Cerf, 1959), pp. 208–11. See below, Chapter 8.

5. See below, Chapter 6.

6. Martin Buber's I-Thou philosophy (In *I and Thou*, trans. Walter Kaufman, 2nd ed. [New York: Scribner's, 1970]) is deficient here, as it does not describe the "We" which results from the "I-Thou" encounter. But one may wonder if this deficiency is not congenital with all non-Trinitarian concepts of God. Ultimately, human persons cannot be "we" if God is not "we." See Tavard, *Woman in Christian Tradition* (Notre Dame, Ind.: University of Notre Dame Press, 1973), pp. 187–210.

7. Paul Tillich, *The New Being* (New York: Charles Scribner's Sons, 1955), p. 32.

8. Plato, in *Great Dialogues of Plato* (New York: NAL, 1956), pp. 101–06.

9. Martin D'Arcy, *The Meeting of Love and Knowledge* (New York: Harper, 1957).

10. John S. Mbiti, *African Religions and Philosophies* (New York: Doubleday, 1970).

PART II

God is Love

VI

God's Love and God's Wrath

Investigation of the knowledge of God can proceed along two main avenues of approach. One can raise the mind up a scale of concepts more and more purified of sense-elements, to the affirmation of the existence and attributes of the Creator, or one can evaluate different claims of revelation and, endeavoring to perceive the inner law of God's self-revelation, hope to catch a glimpse of the interior life of God. The first way is analogical and philosophical. Its value rests on the analogy of being. Within the realm of strict analogy (of proper proportionality) the binding force of its conclusion is absolute. The second way, which may be called theological, achieves a progressive penetration into the revelation, illuminating its veiled dimensions. The analogy or—in Jacques Maritain's vocabulary—the super-analogy of faith supports this way of approach: the revelation is a whole, the various parts of which, while distinct within a common pattern of living truth, shed light on one another.

At first sight, the binding force of such a method may not be as obvious as with the more philosophical method. For a comparison of invisible realities is weakened by the imperfections of human insight. Although in itself the mystery of God is perfect and all-holy, neither its expression in human language nor our ontological participation in it are adequate to the mystery. In this world at any rate the known mystery of God—that is, what is known of it—remains unsatiating.

Those who are used to philosophical or to scientific reasoning may find themselves at a loss in the theological reflection on the question of God. The scholastics arrive at the notion of God through a progressive purification of concepts drawn from the abstractions that follow sensory perceptions. As a result, they exclude from the known attributes of God all qualities that seem to imply a necessary connection with sense-life. They deny, in particular, that God's attributes are analogous to our passions and feelings. Yet the biblical language often refers to God in comparative ways that can hardly be called strict analogies. It speaks, for instance, of God's anger, the "wrath of God," of fire-and-brimstone preaching. Is this a proper way of speaking? What connection is there between love and wrath in God? The Scriptures speak both of the love of God and of his wrath. If love truly belongs in God as an integral aspect of the divinity, is anger a mere metaphor, useful for primitive minds but useless for a constructive criticism of our knowledge of God?

◆ ◆ ◆ ◆ ◆

The prophets encountered the holiness of God. Yahweh, the Lord of Israel, the One who Comes, passed a covenant with the patriarchs, binding them to a life of witness to his own holiness. He came to Abraham as a friend and he remained friend to Abraham's descendants. Yet it was not long before God was known through fear as well as through friendship. After his dream at Bethel, Jacob felt the experience of religous awe: "Truly, the Lord is in this spot, although I did not know it . . . How awesome is this shrine!" (Gen. 28:16–17). Jacob then erected an altar. For worship acts as a safeguard in the presence of the numinous. Moses met with God amid the awesome landscapes of the mountains in the desert. The Presence is grasped through thunder and storm; and even the "tiny whispering sound" (1 Kings 19:12) in which God drew near to Elijah, was heard after a "strong and heavy wind," and after an "earthquake" (1 Kings 19:11). These and similar accounts point to God with the help of images drawn from nature and from strong human personalities. God indeed is faithful to his word and he will keep his part of the Covenant, "bestowing mercy down to the thousandth generation, on the children of those who love me and keep my commandments," but he will pursue his enemies, "inflicting punishments for their fathers' wickedness on the children of those who hate me, down to the third and fourth generation" (Exod. 20:5–6).

God's wrath visits the People of Israel when their behavior falls below the standards of obedience that would mirror the holiness of God. Torah itself bristles with detailed injunctions that are to be kept if the People is to remain holy in God's sight. Even after the Hebraic concept of God has become more sophisticated, the prophets, the psalmists, and the authors of the wisdom books still speak of God's wrath against his People. "Will the Lord reject forever and nevermore be favorable? Will his kindness utterly cease, and his promise fail for all generations? Has God forgotten pity?" (Ps. 77:8–10). Punishment is felt in Israel's experience of sin.

God's wrath is for everyone. For everyone bears a curse on account of his ancestors' sins (Ps. 79:8). As the People is united in the covenant (Ps. 103:17) and in the good (Ps. 37:25), so is it one in evildoing. Psalm 37 speaks of both unity in righteousness and unity in wickedness:

"Neither in my youth nor now that I am old, have I seen a just man forsaken nor his descendants begging bread. . . . Criminals are destroyed, and the posterity of the wicked is cut off" (vv. 25 and 28).

In the experience of sin the People of the Old Testament found the meaning of God's anger and the motivation of his vengeance.[1] For neither is the wrath of God arbitrary nor can it be interpreted as purely symbolic. It expresses a radically religious, as opposed to a superstitious, conception of God. Indeed, the Old Testament is filled with anthropomorphic representations, and we should not expect metaphysical accuracy from the Hebrews. Yet the biblical literature offers something deeper than a mere philosophical representation of God. It conveys a religious experience of God as the God of holiness.

The self-sufficiency of God's love follows from his holiness. God's successive choices and elections imply no hesitancy or repentance on his part. What is one and simple in God is perceived as a series of successive and progressive events in this world. God's love is one and unchanging; yet those whom God loves have been selected one by one. Without any other motive than his love or what the Bible calls condescension—God's stooping kindness for humankind—God calls Abraham. This selection is not exclusive, for God does not hate everyone else: he is even disposed to forgive Sodom and Gomorrah, should five just men be found within their walls. The Hebrews, who saw God's love as personal, expressed it concretely as love for a friend. Isaac is chosen. Jacob is chosen. Why is Jacob preferred to his brother Esau? Because God's choice provides its own unaccountable justification. "Was not Esau Jacob's brother? says the Lord: yet I loved Jacob, but hated Esau" (Mal. 1:3). Man counts for nothing in God's choice.

Since God has struck a Covenant with man, he intends it to be faithfully kept. The Law given to Moses must be obeyed. Disloyalty to the Covenant will therefore provoke a reaction in God's holiness. The anger of God stems from his justice. All who oppose the Covenant incur his wrath. In a frightening page of Leviticus God's wrath is implied in the Covenant itself:

> But if you do not heed me and do not keep all these commandments, if you reject my precepts and spurn my decrees, refusing to obey all my commandments and breaking my covenant, then, I, in turn, will give you your deserts. I will punish you with terrible woes—with wasting and fever to dim the eyes and sap the life. You will sow your seed in vain, for your enemies will consume the crop. I will turn against you, till you are beaten down before your enemies and lorded over by your foes. You will take flight though no one pursues you (Lev. 26:14–17).

The depth of the wrath of God gave rise to one of the finest developments in the history of the People. During the exile, when the Hebrews were deprived of their traditional liturgies, of their places of worship, and of their national sovereignty, the wrath of God had been sharply felt. The return to Palestine had occasioned wild expectations which were disappointed by the hardships of the rebuilding of the city. People began to despair again of achieving a true collective friendship with God. In some circles, an affective piety, characterized by a deep desire for the experience of God's love, developed. The Poor of Israel (*'anawim*) were moved to a great extent by the fear of the Lord.[2] God's hatred for the wicked occurs frequently in their hymns and prayers: "The arrogant may not stand in your sight. You hate all evildoers" (Ps. 5:5). "Let the malice of the wicked come to an end, but sustain the just, o searcher of heart and soul, o just God" (Ps. 7:10).

In the perspective of the Poor of Israel, God's wrath inspires humility and adoration. Sin comes to be interpreted spiritually no less than ritually, individually no less than collectively. The sense of God's holiness reveals the extent of man's sin. "Enter not into judgment with your servant, for before you no living man is just" (Ps. 143:2). Belief in God's jealousy deepens the experience of the numinous. It eventually grows into a motive of hope and trust. For if God hates Israel for its wrongdoings, he loves it for his own promise to Abraham. Leviticus affirms Yahweh's fidelity: "Yet even so, even while they are in their enemies' land, I will not reject or spurn them, lest, by wiping them out, I make void my covenant with them; for I, the Lord, am their God" (Lev. 26:44).

The prophets exploit the theme of the Lord's wooing of Israel, the woman who may be faithful or wayward. God must intervene to sanctify the People. And the Poor of Israel trust that God will soon re-create the People's holiness: "My soul waits for the Lord more than sentinels wait for the dawn . . . Let Israel wait for the Lord . . . and he will redeem Israel from all their iniquities" (Ps. 130:6–8).

From God's wrath to fear of God, and then to hope in the divine mercy: such is the itinerary of the Poor of Israel. The pietistic literature preserved in the Psalms reaches the summit of the Old Testament revelation. Within the context of the relationships between Yahweh and his People, it sketches a synthesis of love and wrath in God. It unites God's wrath against the iniquities of the People to his untiring mercy.

At this point, three lines of thought may be discerned.

The main line puts ire and love side by side. Already when Abraham pleaded for Sodom and Gomorrah, God yielded to his prayer. The same notion is found in

Leviticus 26: after a long list of possible punishments, God reaffirms his own fidelity of love. In Exodus 32:11–35, Moses intercedes for the Hebrews. In Numbers 25:10–24, God turns his wrath away from Israel on account of Aaron's grandson. The anger of God is never so great as to hide his mercy.

The prophets are fond of this theme. "Roam the streets of Jerusalem, look about and observe, search through her public places, to find even one who lives uprightly and seeks to be faithful, and I will pardon her" (Jer. 5:1). "Thus I have searched among them for someone who could build a wall or stand in the breach before me to keep me from destroying the land; but I found no one" (Ezek. 22:30).

Yet these attempts at a synthesis remain cumbersome. Neither justice nor love is fairly treated when the one seems to be correcting the other. God cannot be said to suspend judgment on sinners when he looks for a just man in the city. Nevertheless these anthropomorphisms emphasize the quickening of religious sensitivity among the Hebrews. And there is no question that the imperfections of such a synthesis were felt, be it only because a better one was eventually found.

To Ezekiel we owe a striking expression of a second line of thought.[3] His chapter 18 forms a turning point in biblical ethics. The notion of collective retribution is sharply criticized by the prophet: "The son shall not be charged with the guilt of his father, nor shall the father be charged with the guilt of his son. The virtuous man's virtue shall be his own, as the wicked man's wickedness shall be his" (Ezek. 18:20). Since God no longer punishes children for their father's sins, is it not that punishment as such has no value in his eyes? Thus punishment becomes a means to repentance, an invitation, a call, and no longer a condemnation. "Do I indeed derive any pleasure from the death of the wicked? Do I not rather rejoice when he turns from his evil way that he may live?. . . If a wicked man, turning from the wickedness he has committed, does what is right and just, he shall preserve his life. . . . For I have no pleasure in the death of anyone who dies, says the Lord God" (Ezek. 18: 23, 27, 32).

This new conception can be expressed thus: God's wrath shows his mercy, for it aims at the conversion of the sinner. However, this mitigates the former concept of the wrath of God as God's jealousy toward false gods, but it does not entirely supersede it. God's anger is not denied; it is explained better than in the past. One may surmise here that another point in the revelation and understanding of God's wrath is soon to be reached: a clearer knowledge of the nature of divine love would place the problem on another level. Before such a discovery can be made, however, the fundamental conceptions of the Bible need to be purified. The personal God of Abraham, Isaac, and Jacob is the God of a choice, of a self-sufficient love, and of a wrath which, in certain circumstances, expresses his holiness. Ezekiel does not subvert this scheme. The Poor of Israel, the pietists, the psalmists, the apocalyptists, know that God forgives, not for our sake, but for his own. "For your name's sake, o Lord, preserve me" (Ps. 143:11). Some day God will really punish all iniquity. The Day of the Lord will be a day of dread.

A third line of thought seems to have emerged also after the exile. The songs of the Servant of Yahweh feature a person who is the object of God's love and also suffers under God's wrath.[4] These songs seem all the more striking today as we may read into them the story of the Savior. Being read in the Old Testament by Jesus himself, they were presumably taken by him as typical formulations of some aspects of his mission. They are prophetic, whatever their original meaning may have been, in that they were justified by the subsequent event of the death of Jesus.

For the great prophet who composed these poems, the wrath and the love of Yahweh could be, or would be, or perhaps had already been experienced to their utmost by one man, whom he called the Servant. Whether these songs are autobiographical, biographical, or eschatological, they embody the belief in the perfect unity of God's wrath and God's love:

> If he gives his life as an offering for sin, he shall see his descendants in a long life, and the will of the Lord shall be accomplished through him. Because of his affliction he shall see the light in fullness of days; through his suffering, my Servant will justify many, and their guilt he shall bear (Isa. 53:10–11).

If these lines stand at the acme of the Old Testament, it is to be expected that Jesus would include their message in his life and his teaching. The summit of the Old Testament points to a concrete unity of the wrath and the love of God. The religious pathos conveyed by the songs of the Servant implies awe as well as trust. Yahweh is mighty. He purifies as though by fire, precisely when he most loves.

◆ ◆ ◆ ◆ ◆

In his classic study, *Agape and Eros,*[5] Anders Nygren started widespread discussion on the nature of Christian love. He posited a fundamental opposition between the Greek concept of *eros* and the Christian concept of *agape*. *Eros*, by which creatures desire to rise to the level of the Demiurge, hankers after possession. Once it has been purified of sensory elements, it opens out into a mysti-

cal desire of the One, of God. This characterizes pagan
mysticism, especially that of neo-Platonism; and it was
introduced into Christianity as a foreign element. *Agape,*
the love of God in Christ, is on the contrary a giving of
self to God basically uncontaminated by desire. According to Nygren, a strange phenomenon happened in
apostolic times, when Christian love was polluted by no
less a writer than St. John. In John's Gospel and Epistles,
love is strongly tainted with a longing for God, which
Nygren equates with pagan *eros.* Among the most important reactions to Nygren's conceptions, those of Martin D'Arcy are particularly interesting: D'Arcy investigated the necessary union of *eros* and *agape,* concluding
with the notion that, while *agape* is connected with man
as existence, *eros* is bound up with man as essence.
Given the real distinction between essence and existence, *eros* and *agape* must be both united and distinct.[6]

I am convinced that the New Testament makes no real
distinction between love as it is in God and love as it is in
faithful man. Rather, it reveals God as love and the
presence of that love in man. Those who love with *agape*
love in God through Jesus Christ. We do not add from
without a love of our own to the love that is in God. But
God takes us to himself, and as a result we love in God
through grace as we know in God through faith.

On this point, 1 Corinthians 13, which was examined
in Chapter 4, should not be isolated from the remaining
chapters of the Epistle.[7] In the preceding pages, Paul
speaks of love several times: "Which do you prefer, that I
come to you with a rod, or with love and a gentle spirit?"
(4:21). Toward the end of his letter, Paul will say: "Do
everything with love" (16:13). *Agape* is a personal attitude and a principle of action. In 8:1, *agape* strengthens
the brotherhood: "Whereas knowledge inflates, love

up-builds." It implies an experience of God, and it keeps the community together.

Chapter 13 warns against misuse of extraordinary charisms. Love ought rather to be sought; and it is even more important than faith and hope. Only from the accompanying love do special gifts draw their value. It is also love which lies at the root of the moral virtues (13:4–7). Finally, alone of all virtues, love achieves its perfection in this life and it will outlast the present life together with faith and hope.

Whereas Paul contemplates the love of Christ for men and men's experience of it and response to it, John views love in God himself: "Love, then, consists in this: not that we have loved God, but that he has loved us and has sent his son as an offering for our sins" (1 John 4:10). Love is in us only because God "loved us first" (4:19). The heart of the Johannine message is therefore that "God is love" (4:16). This opens the way to a view of God's life as unfolding itself in a mystery of love. Because Jesus has fellowship with the Father in love, man as believer has fellowship with Christ in God: "I living in them, you living in me," Jesus says to the Father (John 17:23). And: "He who abides in love abides in God and God in him," is John's commentary (1 John 4:16).

Agape is thus conceived to be creative of unity. In God it is oneness; between God and humankind it is union. There is more insistence on the cohesion of this unity than on its structure. But the beginning of St. John's Gospel points to both cohesion and structure: "In the beginning was the Word. . . In him there was life"[8] (John 1:1, 4). Which I take to mean, in the language of slightly later theology: In the Father was the Son; in the Son was the Spirit. All three are, together, *agape*. As to the faithful, they are related to the Three, from whom they receive the gift of the Spirit, which is light: "And life was the light of men" (1:5).

Our awareness of God as love opens a vista into God and also into man's inner life. In man, love participates in God's love. Yet the core of God's love, its intimate nature, remains hidden. Although we experience its presence, we cannot fully analyze its structure. Should we attempt to reach deeper into it, we might well meet with the rebuke, which was also a revelation, that was opposed to Moses' searching questions to God: "I am who am" (Exod. 3:14) or "I am what I am."

Yet the Johannine conception of unity is highly positive; it is more cataphatic than apophatic.[9] Through *agape* we are one with one another and with God, as the Son and the Father are one: "I living in them, you living in me—that their unity may be complete" (John 17:23). It was precisely this mystical dimension of Christian love which Nygren wanted to reject, because he took too literally the Lutheran conception of "imputed righteousness."[10] But in the New Testament taken as a whole, *agape* and mystical *eros* do not contradict each other. They are implied in each other even though we may have to apprehend their togetherness on the pattern of the "coincidence of opposites." Human love for God is no other than God's own love making itself present in man. It desires what God's love wills to give. The apparent dualism of *agape* and *eros* is already resolved in the New Testament. Love unites the faithful to God, since the very essence of the divine life entails oneness in love.

Thus the revelation of *agape* follows some of the lines of the Old Testament. The unity between God and Israel, which had been the aim of the covenant, was finally achieved when Jesus abolished Torah by exhausting its fulfillment. The revelation of God's love as *chesed* was propaedeutic of the revelation of Christ's *agape*.

◆ ◆ ◆ ◆ ◆

The doctrine of God's wrath as inherited from the Old Testament did not arouse theoretical objections among the writers of the New Testament. Yet it could have run foul of the spiritual experience which, being centered on the descent of God into the flesh and his suffering for the sins of humankind, did away with the older imagery of the vengeance of God. Whence the New Testament does not stress the wrath of God. Nevertheless, several passages do imply a doctrine concerning it. The first Epistle of John suggests that sin is impossible for those who are in Christ:[11] "The man who remains in him does not sin. The man who sins has not seen him or known him" (1 John 3:6). "No one begotten of God acts sinfully because he remains of God's stock; he cannot sin, because he is begotten of God" (3:9). The principle of Christian sinlessness is thus clear: grace excludes sin. Sin implies the intrusion into the soul of an element that does not proceed from God. The seed of God which we call grace marks the start of a life of perfect holiness. As such, Christian life excludes sin. Yet, in the exact measure in which the faithful are not yet completely in Christ, they can still fall into sin: "If we say, 'We have never sinned,' we make him a liar and his word finds no place in us" (1:10).

In these conditions one may wonder if the sinlessness of redeemed life should not exclude all notion of the wrath of God. How could God be angry against the holy? Indeed, insofar as we participate in divine love, there is no room in us for any conceivable objects of God's wrath. In the regime of grace all has become love. "Love has no room for fear; rather, perfect love casts out all fear. And since fear has to do with punishment, love is not yet perfect in one who is afraid" (4:18).

Yet, if fear of God has thus been eliminated from life in

love for God, one cannot forget all conception of the
wrath of God. There is still a Day of Judgment. "Our love
is brought to perfection in this, that we should have
confidence in the Day of Judgment" (4:17). Confidence
needs to be instilled in us precisely because the Day of
Judgment remains a day of wrath. Thus John has to draw
a theoretical line in humankind between those who have
God's love in them and those who, being deprived of it,
are the objects of God's wrath. Likewise, the antithetical
framework of Johannine thought divides humankind
between darkness and light. These two never meet, except in the ultimate victory of light over darkness, which
is achieved in Christ. Seen on the background of biblical
realism, this antithesis implies a doctrine of God's wrath.

While he avoids dwelling on the objective aspects of
sin, John draws attention to the subjective plight of sinners. "There is such a thing as a deadly sin; I do not say
that one should pray about that" (1 John 5:16). Deadly
sin implies ultimate alienation from Christ. Before such a
sin, the believer abides in righteousness; through it, the
believer becomes anti-Christ. Anti-Christ is whoever
acts against Christ, whether this is a human person, or
"the world," or "the father of lies." John is emphatic that
anti-Christ is already loose in the world: "Every spirit
that acknowledges Jesus Christ come into the flesh belongs to God, while every spirit that fails to acknowledge
him does not belong to God. Such is the spirit of the
anti-Christ which, as you have heard, is to come; in fact,
it is in the world already" (1 John 4:2–3). To be anti-Christ
means to be caught in the Evil One. "The man who sins
belongs to the devil, because the devil is a sinner from
the beginning" (3:8). It is even possible to extend this
idea further. The world itself, when separated from
Christ, is the realm of the Evil One. In such a world the
faithful know that they are saved because God is their

Father: "We know that we belong to God, while the whole world is under the evil one" (5:19). The prayer of Jesus in chapter 17 of the Johannine Gospel should be read in this perspective: "For these I pray—not for the world . . . I do not ask you to take them out of the world, but to guard them from the evil one. They are not of the world, any more than I belong to the world" (John 17:9, 15–16). God's wrath, in the Johannine perspective, is precisely God's judgment on the Evil One. It will be the task of the Paraclete to make this judgment manifest: "When he comes, he will prove the world wrong about sin, about justice, about condemnation. About sin—in that they refuse to believe in me; about justice—from the fact that I go to the Father and you can see me no more; about condemnation—for the prince of this world has been condemned" (John 16:9–11).

As is suggested in this text, the life of the Church—that span of time between the coming of the Lord and the judgment of the Paraclete—is already a time of judgment. Christ came at the fullness of time. The future will bring about the consummation, on the Day of the Lord. Between preparation and climax there takes place what is both a continued preparation and an anticipated judgment. While the Church witnesses to Christ, the Spirit in the Church judges and condemns the world. This is why John's version of the message of Jesus includes condemnation as well as salvation: "The father you spring from is the devil . . . He brought death to man from the beginning, and has never based himself on truth. Lying speech is his native tongue; he is a liar and the father of lies" (John 8:44).

To sum up, the wrath of God is no less real for John than it is in the Old Testament. It is directed against those who make themselves anti-Christ through the sin unto death, after the fashion of the Evil One who is the prince of this world. The wrath of God is already at work through the Paraclete who anticipates the Day of Judgment. As children of light, the faithful need not fear God's wrath, for they bear the witness of God's *agape* in themselves. Yet they may still feel humility and thanksgiving before God's wrath: humility because they have been redeemed from sin; thanksgiving, because the blood of Jesus has taken them out of the world.

◆ ◆ ◆ ◆ ◆

At the heart of the New Testament, the *agape* of God constitutes the focal point of the Christian community and of the Christian conception of the world and of life. The Old Testament insights that do not fit the belief and trust that God is love are left out of the new horizon of faith. But among the insights that are preserved, although with considerable modifications, one finds the notion of God's wrath.

The wrath of God is the topic of the first part of Paul's Epistle to the Romans.[12] Paul reviews the state of mankind before and after justification through Christ. Before justification, both the heathen and the Jews were steeped in ignorance and sin. The Jewish world was acquainted with the beginning of justification, since the righteousness eventually to be achieved in Christ was already imputed to Abraham through faith. Imputed justice is only temporary. It lasts until the gift of righteousness comes to humankind through the death and resurrection of Christ. After justification, those who participate in Christ through faith and baptism have the justice of Christ in themselves. This is no longer mere imputation. It is their own justice insofar as they are members of the body that Christ is building to himself. Whence the four stages in the history of humankind: paganism (Rom. 1:18–2:11), Law and death (2:12–3:20), imputed justice (3:31–4:25), righteousness in Christ (5–9). Within this last period there is a time of patience, coinciding with the life of the Church, and the eschatological Day of the Lord.

The wrath of God has its place in relation to this religious history of man. Before justification everything lies collectively in the power of sin and death, whether through ignorance as in paganism or by transgression as in Judaism. Thus everything falls under the wrath of God. "The wrath of God is being revealed from heaven against the irreligious and perverse spirit of men who, in this perversity of theirs, hinder the truth" (Rom. 1:18). The situation of Judaism is plain: having received Torah, it has sinned against it. As for the pagans who did not receive the Law, they sinned also against the knowledge of God instilled in their hearts. "In fact, whatever can be known about God is clear to them; he himself made it so. Since the creation of the world, invisible realities, God's eternal power and divinity, have become visible, recognized through the things he has made" (1:19–20). Because pagans have worshipped idols, God abandoned them to themselves. The conclusion is clear: "We have brought the charge against Jews and Greeks alike that they are under the domination of sin" (3:9). "The whole world stands convicted before God" (3:19). Paul sums it up in his Epistle to the Ephesians:[13]

> You were dead because of your sins and offenses, as you gave allegiance to the present age and to the prince of the air, that spirit who is even now at work among the rebellious. All of us were once of their company; we lived at the level of the flesh, following every whim and fancy, and so by nature deserved God's wrath like the rest (Eph. 2:1–3).

After justification, humankind is no longer under God's wrath. "There is no condemnation for those who are in

Christ Jesus" (Rom. 8:1). Christ is the new Adam, the type and model of humankind. He has lifted the wrath of God from the collectivity of men and women, although individuals can still live in a state of sin and condemnation. At this point, two perspectives converge. On the one hand, condemnation has been lifted. On the other, there remains the possibility that the faithful can fall again under the wrath of God. Note Paul's advice to the Corinthians to banish a sinner from the community, handing him over to Satan "for the destruction of his flesh, so that his spirit may be saved on the day of the Lord" (1 Cor. 5:5). But wrath is now mitigated by "forbearance" (Rom. 3:26). The forbearance of God during Israel's history is still at work in God's dealings with the Christians who sin. Wrath admits of mercy. It is a pedagogical anger aiming at conversion rather than at punishment.

Diverse manifestations of God's anger correspond to the successive periods of history. To paganism and to Torah there corresponds a generic anger; to the time of justification a potential anger; in the ultimate period, at the Day of Judgment, there will be a day of fear along the lines of the Old Testament. The wrath of God is an eschatological reality that falls upon all, except those who have been saved by the Lord Jesus, "who delivers us from the wrath to come" (1 Thess. 1:10).

Paul's doctrine may be reduced to simple terms. Christ transfers human persons, through faith, from the power of evil to the kingdom of God. The wrath of God is God's rebuke on evil, and it is felt by humanity insofar as its members still belong to evil. This wrath was manifest before the coming of Christ, when the whole of mankind lived under the power of evil. It will be manifest again at the last day, when the ultimate indictment of evil will be proclaimed. In between, we live in the time of divine forbearance.

Paul's theology bears a striking resemblance to that of John, in spite of obviously different accents. Christians are both sinless and potential sinners. History is divided into a time of preparation and a time of fullness; and this twofold division happens twice: in the Old Testament and also in the New, where the time of the Church leads to the time of the end, just as the time of the Old Testament led to the time of Christ.

The similarity of these two theologies leads us to the question of interpretation: What is the meaning of God's wrath in the New Testament?

◆ ◆ ◆ ◆ ◆

Both in John and in Paul a basic element emerges: the wrath of God, as a divine repulsion of evil, is always at work. It is experienced by those who reject faith in the Christ who died and rose again for the salvation of the world. Such a notion cannot be explained away as though it corresponded to a primitive notion of the divinity unacceptable in modern times. For both John and Paul present us with highly sophisticated theologies. In these we find both the collective experience of humankind faced with psychological anxiety and moral guilt, and the specifically Christian interpretation of this experience in the light of the death and resurrection of Christ. The real problem is not the philosophical incompatibility of anger and immutability in God, but the coincidence of opposites in the oneness of love and wrath.[14]

The primordial mystery of creation gives existence to spiritual beings whom God plans to unite to himself through intimate knowledge and unrestricted love. Creation is the principle of their existence. Re-creation through the Incarnation of the Word is the principle of their union to God. Everything therefore ought to be referred to Christ. All things are recapitulated in him (cf. Eph. 1:10); and "at Jesus' name every knee must bend in the heavens, on earth, and under the earth" (Phil. 2:10). The place of Christ at the center of the new order of heaven and earth implies that God's wrath is now exercised against those who are anti-Christ. Punishment falls upon those who refuse faith knowingly. The rejection of Christ causes the anger of God to be felt. Those who cannot deny Christ because in the first place they do not know him can still feel God's wrath if they stifle the awareness of God in their heart. If we reject the God of creation, we thereby rebuke the God of interior grace and light. We then sin against the Christ who is present in the God we know. Thus Christ is the supreme arbiter of the divine wrath. The Day of Yahweh, the Day of Wrath is identically the "Day of our Lord Jesus" (2 Cor. 1:14), the "Day of Christ" (Phil. 1:10). The wrath of God against sinners remains among the components of the Christian experience. Yet it is mitigated by God's patience; and it leads those who are willing to repentance and reconciliation.

The definitive wrath, which ends all possibilities of reconciliation, is eschatological. It is experienced as soon as a negative option has been definitively chosen. Yet this wrath of God is not outside of the condemned. It is not an extrinsic punishment, an heteronomous sentence, a condemnation, a judgment imposed from without. Man's exclusion from the radiance of the divine glory is born from man and in man. God's wrath is the repulsion by God of those who prefer darkness to light and refuse to heed the meaning of creation. It is the negative relationship that separates from God those who refuse love and choose to become hatred. Such a person is not in hell; it is hell. [15]

Eschatological anger has its ultimate source in the Trinitarian life. Father and Son meet and compenetrate in the Holy Spirit. Creation is intended to be a free participation in this life. But the person who takes position against *agape* opposes the creative act of God that makes that person to be. The denial of creation by a human person affects that person's ontological structure. Before Christ as the Judge of the world who brings evolutionary time to a full stop, anti-Christ provokes a gesture of repulsion. Christ, the alpha and the omega, the beginning and the end, freezes wrongdoers in their immanent punishment: the solipsist contemplation of evil, the companionship of the Evil One. This is the wrath of God. It originates in the love of the Father for the eternal Son. At the last day, Christ will abandon those who have rejected the Father. Thus wrath is implied in divine love. It is the love of the three Persons as experienced in evil. From the point of view of evil, love can only be seen as wrath.

But God's wrath is not only eschatological. It hangs over humankind. [16] It threatens, in the precise measure in which man does not yield to Christ. Spirit is characterized by the capacity to do good or evil. As a free choice, as a spiritual attitude, sin is beyond the limits of time and space. This is why an action can be good or bad in itself, independently of circumstances or situation. [17] A good action may be vitiated by circumstances; a bad action is forever bad.

Sin aims beyond time and space. It anticipates the eschatological situation of hell. Even so, however, the sinful person is in time and can still cancel the residue of past evil, coming back upon it and renouncing it. In the present state of humankind the wrath of God is experienced gradually. God's wrath is instrumentally at the disposal of God's love. It is *agape* calling to repentance. It is the Trinitarian love as felt by those who are still in sin yet also oriented to God. Christ repeats: "Here I stand, knocking at the door" (Apoc. 3:20). The wrath of God does not change; but its effects do change. It calls sinners away from sin. Likewise, as it overhung humankind before the advent of Christ, God's wrath was but God's love which did not find an answer in creation.

Thus the wrath of God amounts to *agape* as experienced in a situation of sin. It is the sinner's last relationship to love.

◆ ◆ ◆ ◆ ◆

In this way the basic antinomy of our knowledge of God is reconciled. We know God as love and we are aware of him as wrath. These are aspects of the divine love, as seen by friends of God and by sinners. This antinomy bares a paradox: God's love is also wrath. These are two aspects of one reality. God is not static. His love is living. Its effects vary: there is human love for God, and human fear of God, and both are born of divine grace.

The life of God is traditionally expressed in the Trinitarian terms, Father, Son, Spirit. Meditation on God's dealings with humankind through love and wrath calls for contemplation of the mystery of God as Three-in-One. Through God's love we should enter the life of the Three Persons.[18] The antinomies discerned in the manifestation of the divine power interlock in the perfect harmony of the divine simplicity.

Notes

1. On sin in the Old Testament, see Louis Ligier, *Péché d'Adam et péché du monde*, (Paris: Aubier, 1960), Vol. 1.; Bonsirven, *Le Judaïsme palestinien au temps du Jésus-Christ*, Vol. 2, pp. 81–105.

2. A. Causse, *Les Pauvres d'Israel* (Strasbourg: Librairie ISTRA, 1922).

3. G. A. Cooke, *The Book of Ezechiel* (Edinburgh: T. and T. Clark, 1936).

4. The songs of the Servant are in Isa. 42:1–9; 49:1–7; 50:4–11; 52:13—53–12; and 62:1–3. One should add Zech. 12:9–14, which seems to imply similar conceptions. See C. R. North, *The Suffering Servant in Deutero-Isaiah: A Historical and Critical Study* (London: Oxford University Press, 1948); Thomas W. Manson, *The Servant-Messiah: A Study of the Public Ministry of Jesus* (Cambridge: Cambridge University Press, 1961); Morna D. Hooker, *Jesus and the Servant: The Influence of the Servant Concept of Deutero-Isaiah in the New Testament* (London: SPCK, 1956).

5. See above, Chapter 1, with note 16.

6. Martin D'Arcy, *The Mind and Heart of Love* (New York: Holt, 1947).

7. See above, Chapter 4, note 1.

8. Here I depart from the translation of the New American Bible: ". . . whatever came to be in him, found life."

9. Cataphatic means affirmative, "according to light"; apophatic means negative, "according to darkness." The allusion here is twofold. On the one hand, classical theology is acquainted with an "affirmative" way and with a "negative " way of speaking of God (together with an "eminent" way). On the other, Christian mystics differ as to the structure of the highest mystical experience, which some describe as an experience of light and others as an experience of darkness: there are mystics of light, like St. Bonaventure, and mystics of night, like St. John of the Cross. Yet they also tend to unite light and night. See Tavard, "The Light of God in the Theology of St. Bonaventure," *Eastern Churches Quarterly* 8 (1950) 407–17; "The Mystery of the Holy Spirit," *Downside Review* 68 (July 1950) 255–70.

10. On Luther's conception of justification, see Paul Althaus, *The Theology of Martin Luther* (Philadelphia: Fortress, 1966), pp. 224–50.

11. On 1 John, see Spicq, *Agape in the New Testament*, Vol. 3, pp. 246–312.

12. Karl Barth, *The Epistle to the Romans* (1933), 6th ed., trans. Edwin C. Hoskins (Oxford: Oxford University Press, 1968).

13. I take Ephesians to be an authentic Pauline letter. See Markus Barth's *Commentary on Ephesians,* Anchor Bible, Vol. 34 (New York: Doubleday, 1974), Vol. 1, pp. 36–53.

14. On the coincidence of opposites, see Nicholas of Cusa, *De docta ignorantia,* bk. ii, ch. 4; *De visione Dei,* ch. 10: Nicholas of Cusa, *The Vision of God* (New York: Unger, 1960), pp. 45–50.

15. The uneasiness of the contemporary Christian conscience with the notion of hell comes from its having been understood as an arbitrary condemnation to punishment from the outside. But such difficulties fall if hell is understood, not as a place, or even as a punishment or condemnation, but as what persons do become once they have definitively chosen evil as their (false) god.

16. Luther is of course a forceful exponent of the doctrine of God's wrath. See Althaus, *Theology of Martin Luther,* pp. 169–78. But many mystics have also described some aspect of the experience of God's wrath in keeping with the development of spiritual sensitivity. See Pascal's pages on "the mystery of Jesus" (Jacques Chevalier, ed., *Pascal: Oeuvres Complètes* [Paris: Gallimard, 1964], pp. 1312–13). Julian of Norwich is a remarkable exception, with her repeated statement that "it is absolutely impossible that God should be angry" (*Revelations of Divine Love,* trans. James Walsh [St. Meinrad, Ind.: Abbey Press, 1974], ch. 49, p. 129).

17. This points up the shallowness of situational theories of ethics.

18. See Tavard, *Meditation on the Word* (New York: Paulist, 1968). For an attempt to see the world religions in Trinitarian perspective, see Tavard, *La Religion à l'épreuve des idées modernes* (Paris: Centurion, 1970), pp. 91–111.

VII

The Incarnation of Love

The revelation of the Tri-Unity upholds the absolute transcendence of God. For God would have been perfectly closed in upon himself had he not turned to creation in a love that was to go as far as the Incarnation and the death on the Cross. When the prophets spoke in the name of the jealous God, who brooks no infidelity in his People, they announced the wrath to come. This was for them a crushing responsibility and a permanent source of trouble. If the authors of the historical books enjoyed telling the tale of long-past chastisements, the prophets were naturally more reluctant to utter present threats. "Burden of Yahweh," "Word of Yahweh" are often prelude to threatening oracles. Yet, however quietly the prophets would have liked to live, they did not fail to deliver their message. God is great; he is transcendent. We still sense his jealousy in Jesus' challenge: "Can any one of you convict me of sin?" (John 8:46).

Sin is precisely the occasion for the jealousy of God. For it is idolatry, the setting up of false gods over against the only true one.[1] Transgression trespasses against God's unicity; it implies worship of an idol hidden in a corner of one's heart. And since in the economy of grace it is truer than ever that man is the temple of God, how could the Holy One accept idols in his temple? How

105

could he let the "abomination of desolation" reign in the Holy of Holies? One must choose between God and Baal. But whereas opting for God can only occasion blasphemies on the part of the father of lies, murderer from the beginning, choosing Baal brings in its wake the jealousy of God.

The preceding chapter examined some aspects of God's love and wrath. The Old Testament remains up to date on this question. If God was indeed jealous when the Incarnation was being prepared, how much more jealous should he not be, now that his Son has assumed humankind as his own body, and his Spirit lives in the hearts of men and women! One may still speak of the jealousy of God. Not that this will frighten people into a virtuous life. The preaching that attempts it is as ineffective as it is undistinguished. What is needed is a sense of awe, a sense of worship.

The Cross symbolizes the Christian faith. The sign of the Cross testifies that we believe in redemption through the Cross. St. Justin read the Cross as a natural sign, present all over the pagan world, of the truth of the Gospel. One may wonder, however, whether to the average Christian, the Cross evokes suffering or victory: Does it connote the self-sacrifice of Jesus for the sins of the world or the triumph of his resurrection? Several interpretations of the mystery of Golgotha are possible: Did Christ die as a result of an eternal decree? Had it been decided from all eternity that he should incur the jealousy of God in the name of sinners? Or did he make atonement the form of the historical redemption because he knew that his people would put him to death? Did he take flesh in order to die on the Cross? Or did he suffer that kind of death as a result of an historical accident, the blundering of the Jewish leaders?[2]

◆ ◆ ◆ ◆ ◆

Asked pointblank, the last question cannot fail to provoke a negative answer. The Christian instinct wisely
rejects all tendencies to build up an opposition between
God and Jesus. Being the Word of God, Jesus can hardly
have contradicted himself: There can be no real strain
between the divine and the human, which were perfectly harmonized by coinherence in the Word. This is
implied in the doctrine of the Council of Chalcedon. Yet
the conclusions to be drawn therefrom can go more or
less far, and the Passion can still be conceived as more or
less accidental to the mission of Jesus.

The Passion may have been a contingent event that
would have been entirely left out of our Lord's earthly
career had the Jewish people as a whole acknowledged
his mission. Through their failure, redemption became a
suffering and the Cross was made the symbol of the new
order of things: mankind saved in spite of its chosen
representatives.

This view enhances the meaning of the Cross: mankind is saved in spite of itself. The instrument of the
rejection of Christ becomes the gate of salvation. The
Passion is less a mystery of suffering than it is one of
love. And when we say, "Christ died for our sins," we
express not so much the essence of his mission, which
was to reveal the life of God, as the meaning acquired by
his death.

Many passages of the New Testament are thrown into
sharp light by this point of view. The life purpose of Jesus
is expressed in the exclamation: "O Jerusalem,
Jerusalem, murderess of prophets and stoner of those
who were sent to you! How often have I yearned to
gather your children, as a mother bird gathers her young
under her wings, but you refused me" (Matt. 23:37). The

episode at Nazareth, when Jesus evokes the image of the Servant of Yahweh, may correspond to Jesus' hope that his countrymen would accept him. One senses a foretaste of failure in the words: "No prophet is without honor except in his native place, indeed in his own house" (Matt. 13:57).

Christian tradition has always understood the Passion and the Resurrection as the Lord's victory over death and sin. The glory of the resurrected body of Christ already shines forth from the Cross. On Good Friday, the Church looks forward to Easter Sunday. And the faithful are baptized in both the death and the resurrection of the Lord. Rising from the tomb with the sun of Easter morning, Christ is *vir oriens,* the man rising in the East, who gives life like the sun. He rose with the rising sun; he ascended to heaven toward the East (Ps. 67:34), from where he is expected to come back. This seems to have been the primal meaning of the cross which adorns Christian homes: it was originally placed on the east side of the house or the room, indicating the direction from which the Son of Man will come again, bearing the marks of his glorious passion.

Orthodox Christianity has developed this awareness of the glory of Christ more than the West has done.[3] The typical Byzantine church is dominated by a mosaic of the Lord of glory, the Christ *Pantocrator,* to whom all power has been given in heaven and on earth. Thus, the fundamental Christian attitude seems to unite joy and awe. Piety stresses baptism in the death and resurrection of the Lord. Significantly, Theodore of Mopsuestia spoke of Christ taking hold of the host at the consecration as he took hold of his body again at the resurrection. The resurrection is the archetype of all Christian realities. Its virtue has transformed the world.

In general the Johannine writings warn against too

ethereal a conception of the Incarnation and they use all occasions to counteract docetism. Still and all, the Cross appears as a throne rather than as gallows. The crucified Jesus is not so much tortured as lifted up, that all may behold him and be saved, as all were saved who looked at the serpent lifted up by Moses. The ascension which crowns Jesus' life begins with his raising on the Cross. Christ looks forward to it as to a rallying point: "And I—once I am lifted up from earth—will draw all men to myself" (John 12:32). It will open the eyes of his disciples: "When you lift up the Son of Man, you will come to realize that I AM" (John 8:28). Thus the Cross has been transformed into an instrument of glory. He who is the Word (John 1:1), the Light (John 1:9), the Name (John 1:12), the Glory (John 1:14) is also the Life (John 6:35). His historical death is therefore clothed with a meaning that makes it into a triumph. The Apocalypse (1:6) identifies the Christ who was lifted up with the "Man in the clouds" of the Danielic tradition. Christ has divine power and his death entitles him to glory: "I am the First and the Last, and the One who lives. Once I was dead but now I live—forever and ever" (Apoc. 1:17–18).

The Johannine contemplation of the mystery of Christ tends to visualize the passion in the light of subsequent events. The glorious uplifting of Jesus is the crowning point of his career. It is seen in the light of his resurrection, his ascension, and his reign in heaven.

A similar emphasis in the Epistle to the Hebrews sets forth the death of the Lord as his passage to the heavenly priesthood: "For the sake of the joy which lay before him, he endured the cross, heedless of its shame. He has taken his seat at the right hand of the throne of God" (Heb. 12:2). Through suffering, he intercedes perfectly as the high priest of the New Law. "Son though he was, he learned obedience from what he suffered; and when perfected he became the source of eternal salvation for all who obey him, designated by God as high priest according to the order of Melchizedek" (Heb. 5:8–10).

We may understand the fourth word from the cross in the same perspective: *"Eli, Eli, lama sabachthani?"* It is a hymn to the glory of God, the Lord intoning a psalm to worship the Father at this supreme moment. Far from being a sign of bitterness or the cry of human anguish, it would convey the unbelievable joy that fills the heart of Jesus. Praising God in his death, Jesus the Christ fulfilled the antitype of Job: "The Lord gave and the Lord has taken away: blessed be the name of the Lord!" (Job 1:21).

If the passion is thus spiritualized, this should by no means be the chief aspect of New Testament teaching. Other elements should be held in mind for a balanced view of the mystery of the Incarnation. Christ crucified is "the power of God and the wisdom of God" (1 Cor. 1:24); and Paul never softens the shocking fact that the Savior died on a cross. Though to pagans it means "absurdity" and it is "a stumbling block" to Jews, Christian piety vindicates for the Cross the privilege of being the instrument of salvation. A medieval hymn chants: "O Crux, ave, spes unica!" Twenty centuries after being erected outside the Holy City, the Cross still appeals to those who thirst after justice and it symbolically points to heaven. The uplifting of Jesus took place at the end of the way of sorrows.

"Your attitude must be that of Christ: Though he was in the form of God, he did not deem equality with God something to be grasped at. Rather, he emptied himself and took the form of a slave, being born in the likeness of men. He was known to be of human estate, and it was thus that he humbled himself, obediently accepting even death, death on a cross" (Phil. 2:5–8). This text brings complementary light to bear on the Passion. The death on the cross was the outcome of the free choice by which, after eluding several attempts at murder, Jesus walked to Jerusalem against his friends' advice, stopped the half-hearted endeavor of Peter to defend him with the sword, and gave himself up. He had been looking forward to that event.

Too much stress should therefore not be put on the idea that Jesus fell victim to an obscure transcendental law of suffering, according to which pain would be necessary to forgiveness. Either God forgives or he does not; and if he does, he also condones. The face of things is renewed by divine forgiveness, and subsequent atonement is superfluous. God is Father. His pardon wipes guilt away and there only remain the fact and the memory of having sinned. The notion of the pain due to sin, on which Anselm based his theology of redemption, results from an extrapolation of sacramental practice into the life of God. Yet nothing warrants the legitimacy of that application. The humbling of the Lord, his kenosis, has a far deeper origin in the divine life itself.

According to the kenotic ideal in Russian spirituality, the pattern of Christian holiness would be to practice a material and spiritual poverty reaching unto abasement;[4] utter destitution supported for Christ would be the touchstone of man's identification with him. If Christ took the form of the Servant, would not servanthood, or nonresistance to evil, typify Christian sanctity? This view does not emphasize an imitation of Christ's patience, a moral behavior. It rather points to an ontological mystery: in Christ and therefore in the Church and in all its members, a kenosis is achieved in which the higher realities hide in the lower.[5] The recapitulation of all takes place, not in the elevation of the world toward God, but in the descent of God into the world. Man belongs to an intermediate plane between

God and the cosmos. Through him God has willed to accomplish his descent. His personal incarnation forms one phase in the divinization of all, the first stage being creation and the third being the life of the Church. Non-resistance to evil is thus integrated in a Christian out-look. The Passion and the Cross represent the extent to which Christ has already carried the humility of the Church. All the evil and the suffering of the world were assumed in the human experience of Christ, so that the Church's humiliation shares in Christ's passion: it is Christ who suffers and is humbled in it.

Clearly, not all the elements of the kenotic ideal belong to the same level. A renewal of material creation is part of the Christian hope: "The whole created world eagerly awaits the revelation of the sons of God" (Rom. 8:19). One may doubt that the means to such a renovation should be a progressive self-emptying of God into the lower realities of the created world. A fallacious deifica-tion of the creature would entail a veiling of God's glory. A kenosis understood in too gross a fashion would leave little room for the sanctification of mankind which is the aim of the Incarnation.

Rather than look at man as part of a cosmos destined to be divinized by grace, we should consider the world as assumed in man's nature and worship. The kenosis of the Word aims at transforming man and ensuring a pro-gressive sublimation of the world as a result. Through this companionship with the Mystical Body, material creation will experience the manifestation of the children of God. There is no self-emptying of God and of man into the cosmos. On the contrary, there is an assumption of the cosmos into man and God. It is on the level of the spiritual creature that the aim of the Incarnation is to be found.

At this height, however, the kenosis of Christ going to

the Cross makes sense. Christ tied his mystical body to himself by living its life beforehand. Besides being his own historical pilgrimage along the paths of Palestine, Jesus' life was also a sacramental rehearsal of the Church's life through all ages. He promised to remain with the Church until the end of the world. Yet with the end of his human life upon earth, the end of time had already been reached mystically. As well as a prophecy, his promise was a conclusion, the recalling of what had taken place. He "who is, who was, and who is to come" (Apoc. 1:8) concentrated in himself the subsequent existence of the Church. The moment of his coming was the "designated time" (Gal. 4:4), precisely because his Person lived both through time and in eternity. The meeting point of two radically diverse modes of being, dimensional and instantaneous, temporal and eternal, coupled the eternal life of his divine Person with the historical succession of his physical and mystical body. In the human Christ the mystical body was what it is now in the course of its historical development. At the end of history it is due to reach eternity again through a second experience of divine descent into history at the second coming.

From this point of view it seems that Christ willed to undergo the different states of his mystical body and first of all its physical and moral sufferings. The spiritual life of the Church was present in his prayer; its missionary activities were alluded to in the preaching of the gospel; its sufferings were also borne. "He emptied himself and took the form of a slave, being born in the likeness of men. He was known to be of human estate, and it was thus that he humbled himself, obediently accepting even death, death on a cross" (Phil. 2:7–8). Accordingly, the function of the Mystical Body does not essentially consist in patterning its life upon the Passion of Christ. Rather, its own passion has already been undergone by its Head who has triumphed over suffering. "Take courage! I have overcome the world" (John 16:33). The kenosis of Christ identified him with the suffering members of his mystical body.

This view of the Passion is in keeping with the Johannine and the Byzantine views of the glory of the human Christ. The Cross has two aspects. Connected with Christ as God Incarnate, it is a throne, an uplifting, a symbol and instrument of glory, a preliminary phase of the ascension. Connected with Christ as assuming mankind, it is a symbol of humility under the weight of which the Lord stoops down to meet the poorest of his disciples. At the crossroad of two traditions, therefore, this should solve the question raised: Did the suffering Jesus fall victim to the jealousy of God?

Evidently, the Son of the eternal Father could on no account become the object of God's wrath. No idol, no anti-God, no anti-Christ could be found in him. The holy humanity of the Lord, being the most perfect work of creation, could not be defiled by sin. In no way could it be made odious to the Father.

What happened in the Passion, then, was that Christ experienced in his soul and his body the apparent dereliction of the Church and mankind in some periods of history. The Church suffered in Jesus; the faithful had their sins and failures visited in the humanity of the Incarnate Word through his assumption of their purifying trials. The Lord was indeed not punished by the jealousy of the living God; but he took everything upon himself. "For we do not have a high priest who is unable to sympathize with our weakness, but one who was tempted in every way that we are, yet never sinned" (Heb. 4:15). Jesus was not hidden under the sins of the world; he did not become, by substitution, an object of horror for his Father, forsaken and left to die. The kenosis was of another kind, deeper in the unity it achieved with the suffering members of the Mystical Body, better in keeping with the mystery of love which is the motive of the Incarnation and the very life of the Trinity: it was the mystical assumption of the trials of the Church in the human nature of its Head.

Once again, this opens a perspective on the life of God as love. Only love as the very substance of God could proceed to such an identification with mankind. We are thus referred back to the basic paradox of the notion of God: God is at the same time absolute and living. As absolute he is the All-Other, having nothing in common with man. As living he is love and relates to human-kind, whose life is also, at each stage, a form of love.

◆ ◆ ◆ ◆ ◆

The problem has now been pushed back. It is not Jesus, but men who incur the jealousy of God. There are trials in which one experiences, in the words of Bernanos, "that the most inhuman of man's passions finds its ineffable image in Him and that, as the ancient Jews divined without understanding, He is a jealous God."[6] The sum of the various tests that are undergone on earth constitutes the suffering life of the Church. The most purely spiritual of these will help us to understand the others. Such are the mystical purifications.[7]

The mystical purifications are not sensational events. They should not be looked upon as elements of a special and mysterious kind of drama. No more than any other renouncement are they mysterious. In some form or other they furnish the daily bread of all fervent Christians. God hides himself from man; this is the essence of the mystical purifications. And in so doing, God presents us with a new way to give up lingering forms of spiritual idolatry. Like all other purifications, they attempt to deepen man's basic freedom to such a degree that one will forsake all that is not the will and the presence of God.

I am not concerned here with giving a technical account of the various kinds of purifications, "actual" and "passive," "of senses" and "of spirit." These are distinguished according to the differing means that bring them about. They do not only bear on sins or evil actions, ideas or feelings; they also strip man of accretions, both bad and good, and lay him bare and defenseless before the Lord. Spontaneously, we build up a front line of habits, likes and dislikes, hopes and memories, thick enough to sieve out unknown elements that might reach consciousness. God, even to the faithful, is radically unknown. He is a Power behind everything, whom one knows about and loves in a way, but whom one is reluctant to come near to. The religions, whether false or true, have developed rituals and dogmas. As well as expressions and means of communion, these are barriers between God and man. For a unity which has been projected into words falls short of the perfect oneness that experience alone will reveal. Christianity achieves a perfect penetration of the divine into the human. Its dogmas and rites are God-given: God breaks through them into our consciousness.

The penetration of God to the center of man's personality, where no veil can come in between, is incipient in faith. However, it cannot attain to perfection as long as the personality is divided. Man must eventually be entirely imbued with God. God is here already by grace through faith. Yet awareness of his presence is hindered by the trick through which our usual self-knowledge does not furrow deeper than the surface of consciousness. We need to be disencumbered. Provided one is willing, God will take upon himself to bring the task to a finish. Properly speaking, this divine taking over of man's consciousness coincides with the mystical purifications: these are "nights" at the end of which nothing should remain to be seen, felt, and rested in, except the fire of God himself. All this does not take place without profound spiritual anguish, for it is alien to natural likes.

The subjective attitude of this inward night is summed up in the notion of "abandonment." John Ruysbroeck notices that a person undergoing spiritual purification eventually reaches the brink of despair. Being deprived of all felt presence of God, when, as far as can be done, all idols have been destroyed, he finds himself in an unforeseen barrenness. To all appearances he is abandoned by God, and has actually reached "the extreme point in which he can live outside despair." Abandonment into the hands of God can alone open the way out of this plight. "Man will abandon himself in all things, saying and thinking in his heart: . . . Lord, it is not my will according to nature which must be fulfilled, but thy own will and my will according to the spirit. Lord, because I am thine and because, if thy glory were at stake, I would go to hell as willingly as to heaven, do with me what will bring glory to thee."[8]

This explains the nature of abandonment. It is not despair. It entails no adherence to evil, despair being essentially a refusal of forgiveness. Nor is it indifference to God's glory. It is hope, but it does not use the object of hope as a crutch. The final end of man is not man's happiness; it is God. To expect one's own transformation or predestination amounts to making a means into an end, to subdue God to our service. On the contrary, to trust God with no thought for, though no exclusion of, beatitude, does full justice to the Absolute God.

This points out the positive nature of abandonment

and of the purifying nights. Were it to lead to indifference, abandonment would be negative. But nothing is more positive than to acknowledge the transcendence of God. This is at the heart of all genuine religion and at the basis of all true worship. Thus man is enabled to break his highest idols; he comes nearest to beatitude when he least worries about it.

Dereliction is undergone in order that God might be sole master in man. Since God is God, he would contradict himself were he to admit rivals. Desiring to communicate himself to mankind, he creates the world and takes flesh in the Christ. His living and loving fire must burn out of man all impediments to perfect communion. The proper function of his jealousy is to achieve this purification. It is the more exacting and far-reaching as the impossibility of a genuine rival reveals the possibility for the heart of man to harbor idols: not gods, only dressed up knick-knacks, bit by bit filling all the inside of man. God is jealous because he creates minds able to make their own choice; in other words, because he is Love.

By love, God purifies man till he becomes the Being of man's own choosing, the only object of worship. Out of love, Christ takes upon himself the sufferings of his Mystical Body. All this constitutes the mystery of the jealous love of the Father.

In this wise, the fact of suffering is essential to human creatureliness. The common explaining away of physical evil and suffering as being a lesser kind of good and therefore no evil at all, a mere absence of being, appears at this point to be unsatisfactory. The philosophical world outlook of which it is part fails to grasp the positive nature of suffering; it considers suffering from the outsider's point of view, in the conditions that make it possible. A profounder view should start from a reflection on the experiential meaning of suffering. There only can it be appreciated in its concrete complexity, outside of which it is no more than an abstraction.

Suffering as an experience of self does not exist outside the spiritual world. It is a mark of spiritual existence. Only such an experience of self may be judged otherwise than in the abstract. The possibility of a solution to the problem of pain is thus opened.

A purely objective solution will not do. For it would overlook the subjective aspect of self-experience through suffering. Insofar as they are part of a spiritual history, all things are subjective. Now man's physical and moral suffering issues into a spiritual freedom where the soul is stripped of the artificial weight of the social and physical themes that crowd in his consciousness. Accepted suffering lifts man up from the plane of habit to the solitude of intimacy with God. By veiling all else, spiritual suffering awakens to a higher sphere of life. It gives a warning that God is approaching. It is a gift from God where the climax of love is reached in the mystical nights. To these all suffering is ordained.

Suffering is better than an absence. It is a presence, the anticipated presence of God yet to come and preparing his entrance. Physical evil, necessary as it is to corporal and sometimes to moral suffering, is not merely a lesser good. As a relative good, it draws its goodness and therefore its positivity from what it is related to. Man makes relative good highly positive when he accepts it and thereby transforms himself in the expectation of the coming of the Lord; or he turns it into evil when he refuses it and thereby closes himself to the visitation of God.

◆ ◆ ◆ ◆ ◆

The question of moral evil is thus mooted. Is there such a thing as positive evil? Here again the classical answer appears to be insufficient, because incomplete.

In the two instances we have studied, the passion of Christ and the mystical nights, the jealousy of God had to be defined as an aspect of his love. This can be further precisioned now: jealousy is the function of God's love when it encounters its contradictory. Now the opposite of God is not creation; it is hatred. In the Passion, Jesus experienced the sufferings of mankind, from which, according to the Epistle to the Hebrews, he "learned obedience"; he acquired in his human behavior the attitude which was his in his divine personality. The moral sufferings of mankind arise from a tension between an upward call from God and the downward appeal of a creation that is misinterpreted.

As for the mystical nights, the purifications that take place in them reach to the inner border between sin and good, and they foster a far more accurate knowledge of good and evil than was before. Is this not because all the interior city of man tends of its own weight toward a demonic defiance of the Creator? In a soul which has been deeply purified, consciousness of sin can co-exist with absence of sin: sin passes away, but having sinned remains. And this is enough to make one feel all the weight of one's downward fall.

This brings in the problem of what relation connects mankind with the state of sin in which every man is born, original sin.

The obstacle to God, that which of necessity incurs his jealousy, is a latent or open desire of forging idols for oneself, of denying God his divinity. Man is placed at the junction of matter and spirit, blindness and light, necessity and liberty. The union of these two principles in him is agonistic. Only after long efforts can he master himself. There remains, even then, a potential clash between two tendencies. The Golden Age, whether it is located in the past or in the future, is a dream of human beings who, despite their day by day experience, long for the lasting harmony of self with self. Original sin is no other than the agonistic relation of the two principles in man. Historically—or rather prehistorically—it is a source of sin. Transhistorically it is the seed of all sin. Personally it carries less guilt than any actual sin, since it is not voluntary.[9] Whatever it may have been at the beginning of humankind, its remains and sequels are seen in the fight between the principles of the flesh and the spirit in us.

Is there evil in the case of this original sin, in which all evil originates? This question is all the more important as the nature of man depends on its solution. If there is no intrinsic evil in original sin such as it remains in man, how could there be any evil at all in his life? How, then, could God be a jealous God?

The jealousy of God is no other than his love. In the logic of love the creation of man as capable of sin is compatible with the creative *agape*. Love permits to happen something that it will punish. It permits it because it wants freedom, and the capacity to sin is part and parcel of human freedom.

Spiritual beings are free to stand for what they like. Moral evil will result from the attitude of a man who chooses the lower elements of his nature as against the higher. In final analysis this man decides for idols against God. Man's God-given dynamic virtualities are engaged in such a behavior. Evil is an action that rebounds on its own agent. Good or bad, an action implies a personal commitment, an experience of self on the spiritual level. Since man's essence is naturally ambiguous, it is normal that the choice between God and anti-God, Christ and anti-Christ, should provoke a particularly acute crisis: moral suffering. None can be content with choosing evil; for the experience of such a choice is already biding its time; it is a possibility with unforeseen results. All purity fears impurity. Anticipated fear of evil is already a psychological token of its possibility. It is inseparable from the mystery of creative love. For it results from created freedom, which is the fruit of God's creative love.

Man is thereby directed toward the antimony of good and evil. Man's constitution puts him on the path of moral suffering and possible moral evil. Elimination of the latter cannot be done without painful renouncement. The sum total of all the pains of mankind was mystically assumed by the Incarnate Word: "Word of Yahweh against" every man, for in the course of his purification, each one meets the jealous God before sharing the fruits of his love.

◆ ◆ ◆ ◆ ◆

Hope leaves no doubt that the dream of mankind will come true. Whatever the origin was, the end of the world shall imply a transformation of man's flesh: "the redemption of our bodies" (Rom. 8:23). Man's ambivalence can be superseded by no less than a spiritualization of creation as a whole. When the created world will no longer furnish us with idols, then man's internal strife will be over.

It is significant that the mystery of the jealousy of God should lead us to an optimistic note. Christian optimism, which transcends the naiveté of superficial optimism, embraces all human history. The struggles and sufferings, the illusions and awakenings, the expectations and disappointments of humankind originate in an ontic discrepancy in man himself, the discrepancy of knowledge and will, of subject and object. Their sense is to point to an eschatological achievement offered as a grace. Between creation and its final unification in the Kingdom, there lies the short stretch of history during which God's love expresses itself in jealousy. From the viewpoint of Christian faith, Christianity alone ensures the certainty of the final oneness after which mankind is blindly striving. Deeper than any philosophy, faith reveals the ultimate unity of the spiritual dilemma in which, for the time being, we live. Nothing is negative. The chasm which is open in the heart of man is not yet bridged in the present life; yet through anguish and suffering we are being transmuted by the jealousy of the living God into that image of himself which has been assumed, once and for all, by the Son of Man and was nailed with him to the Cross before being raised in him a spiritual body.

Thus it is that access to the love of God on our part entails a participation in the agony of Christ. The flesh and the spirit are not two principles in man. Each of them is man in his totality; but the flesh is man by himself and the spirit is man as related to God. The experience of suffering love shows man to be, in a sense, one in two, or two experiences in one person. This places man on the way to the mystery of God as Three and One. For our relation to God is twofold. In creation, God made man as flesh, and gave him all. In spiritual union to himself, God makes man as spirit and takes all that man is. We thus end on a twofold paradox, the paradox of man, one and yet torn between flesh and spirit, and the paradox of God, who at the same time gives all and takes all.

Once more, the basic paradox of God comes to light: God is not static, but living. His life is an aspect of his absolute transcendence. And yet the adventure of man as flesh and as spirit is patterned on the divine life. This is the mystery of God as Three and of the Christian's participation in the Triune life.

Notes

1. This notion is basic to the anthropology of Calvin. It has been presented more recently in different forms, by Karl Barth and by Paul Tillich, for example.

2. Besides the classical treatments of redemption, such as Gustav Aulen, *Christus Victor* (New York: Macmillan, 1969); see Jürgen Moltmann, *The Crucified God* (New York: Harper and Row, 1974); Paul Tillich, *Systematic Theology*, 3 vol. (Chicago: University of Chicago Press, 1967), Vol. 2.; G. C. Berkouwer, *The Work of Christ*, Studies in Dogmatic Theology, 9 (Grand Rapids, Mich.: Eerdmans, 1965).

3. John Meyendorf, *Christ in Eastern Christian Thought* (Washington: Corpus, 1969); Alexander Schemann, *The World as Sacrament* (London: Darton, 1966), originally *Sacraments and Orthodoxy* (New York: Herder, 1965).

4. See *The Way of a Pilgrim*, and *The Pilgrim Continues His Way*, trans. Reginald M. French (New York: Seabury, 1965).

5. This view of kenosis varies from the kenotic christologies that have been fashionable in the Anglican theology of this century. See Lewis B. Smedes, *The Incarnation: Trends in Anglican Thought* (Leiden: Brill, 1953).

6. Georges Bernanos, *Joy*, trans. Louise Varèse (New York: Pantheon, 1946), p. 41.

7. This is the topic of St. John of the Cross's basic works, *The Ascent of Mount Carmel* and *The Dark Night*. See *Collected Works*, trans. K. Kavanaugh and O. Rodriguez (New York: Christian Classics, 1973).

8. Jan Van Ruysbroeck, *L'Ornement des noces spirituelles* (Oosterhout: Saint-Paul-de-Wisques, 1915), p. 118.

9. Thomas Aquinas, *Summa theologica*, III, q. 1, a. 4.

VIII

The Three Persons

We have reached the converging points of several lines.
God is love; and yet we can speak of his love meaning-
fully only if we include in it the aspect of wrath. The
Christian revelation is entirely oriented toward this coincidence of two poles, identical yet distinct, in God's love.
This provides a first instance of identity-yet-distinctness
which cannot be avoided if we want to speak of God.

A dramatic example of identity-yet-distinctness is
seen in the Passion of the Lord. Here we touch directly
the paradox of God submitting to the conditions of
human existence; living in the human nature, which the
sin of man crushed; and, having undergone human
agony to the end, reversing the situation and imposing
himself forever as the supreme type of divine-human
victory. In the Passion, Christ shows himself to be identical with God, yet, as he is the recipient of God's love,
distinct from the Father.

Finally, human experience at its highest displays, by
participation, a similar pattern of identity-yet-distinctness. Mystical experience unveils the paradox that God
is both the one who gives all and the one who takes all.
Night becomes light. In this "learned unknowing" of
Pseudo-Dionysios[1] and the medieval mystics,[2] "nothing" is balanced against "all" in a mystical exchange

which has been sung by St. John of the Cross: "Not living in myself I live/And wait with such expectancy/I die because I do not die."[3] At this point, man sees himself to be far from, and yet drawn into, God's life. This infinite distance within participation is modeled on the identity-yet-distinctness which we have discerned in the life of God.

Traditional Christian dogma expresses this paradox in Trinitarian terms.[4] All along I have taken this Trinitarian pattern for granted. I regard the terms Father, Son, Spirit, as being indissolubly connected with the revelation of the Gospel: in Christ God revealed himself as One-in-Three or, conversely, Three-in-One, ineffably self-identical and distinct-from-self. As I understand it, this pattern corresponds to the structure of eternal love.

My whole approach has started from the experience of divine love in the Old and the New Testaments. At each level, love instances identity in distinction. It unites persons, making them one at the very moment when they remain other. Human love unites persons as though each were the other. Such is the meaning of the Gospel saying: "Treat others the way you would have them treat you: this sums up the Law and the Prophets" (Matt. 7:12). We are able so to behave in the measure of our identification with others. Paul draws the relevant conclusion in regard to marital love: "He that loves his wife loves himself" (Eph. 5:28). Marriage unites two in one flesh: "And the two of them become one body" (Gen. 2:24).

The mystery of God as One-in-Three is a mystery of love. God's essence is to love. When he wrote, "God is love" (John 4:8), John formulated the key to Trinitarian theology: God is ineffably distinct from himself. This we call Father and Son: the Father as *being* and the Son as *distinct* from the Father. Yet God is one: this we call the

Spirit, *uniting* the Father and the Son. In this central knot of God's inner life, all other paradoxes are resolved. For they all derive from the ultimate mystery of God's love. In particular, the paradox of God's love in relation to humankind is explained. Already in the prophets, and above all in the Word made flesh, the revelation raises mankind to a participation of God's love and thus to an insight into the plural oneness of God. For this reason the prophets could not perceive God's nearness without seeing his distance also. It is the why and wherefore of the suffering Incarnation: Christ could reveal the friendship of God only in his justice, his nearness only in his distance, the Resurrection only by way of the Cross. But that which is harmonious in God has not been fully reconciled in us. We may know that transcendence and immanence are one, but we do not see it.

◆ ◆ ◆ ◆ ◆

That such is the New Testament picture of God should need no telling. The theophany of Christ's baptism revealed his mission: "He saw the Spirit of God descend like a dove and hover over upon him. With that, a voice from the heavens said: This is my beloved Son. My favor rests on him" (Matt. 3:16). The divine persons are pictorially represented: the One in heaven, the Son on earth, and the Spirit uniting them. A similar image closed the public ministry of Jesus, when the apostles' mission was announced: "Go, therefore, and make disciples of all the nations. Baptize them in the name of the Father and of the Son and of the Holy Spirit" (Matt. 28:19). The entire public life of Jesus is thus enshrined by the Gospels in what may be called a Trinitarian iconography.

The imprint of the divine figures that are both three and one persists through the Epistles. Several Pauline passages speak of Christ in terms of Spirit: "The Lord is the Spirit, and where the Spirit of the Lord is, there is freedom" (2 Cor. 3:17). In others Paul refers to Jesus in terms of God: "Though he was in the form of God, he did not deem equality with God something to be grasped at" (Phil. 2:6). All this is possible granted the basic distinction-in-oneness of the Father, Jesus or the Son, and the Spirit. The reality of the Father belongs also to the Son and the Spirit. What varies is their interrelationship. Within the same divine reality, the Father is not the Son or the Spirit; nor is the Son the Father or the Spirit; nor is the Spirit the Father or the Son. Yet in their relations to what is not themselves, the Three are one reality only: one God, internally plural. "Philip. . . whoever has seen me has seen the Father" (John 14:9). In the theological terms of the Council of Florence, *omnia sunt unum, ubi non obviat relationis oppositio* (everything is one, except where there stands a relational opposition).[5] Referring to this common reality, the tradition uses terms of oneness; pointing to the internal relationships of God, it must employ terms of threeness.

◆ ◆ ◆ ◆ ◆

Christian piety does not demonstrate the Trinity anymore than it proves the incarnation or redemption. It can only develop ways of showing the nonabsurdity of the Trinitarian faith. These ways are purposely negative. They do not establish anything new concerning God. They only tend to prove that distinctions within the unity of the Godhead make sense. One should not therefore expect from Christian theology more than it tries to give. No attempt at rationalizing the Trinity is in keeping with the implications of the revelation. If this were the purpose of the Trinitarian analogies envisaged by theologians, their task would have been vain. As this has never been their aim, it would be equally futile to deny the Trinity on the ground that the analogies that unfold the meaning of Trinitarian formulas do not amount to scientific or philosophical demonstration.

The analogy which fits best with the approach adopted in the present essay is that of love. Love, in human experience, posits two lovers united by mutual love. These correspond to the three divine Figures in such a way that we may consider the Trinity to be the Threeness of the Father, the Son whom he loves, and their reciprocal love, the Spirit. Richard of St. Victor, in the twelfth century, was the great exponent of this analogy.[6] It was used by the scholastics of the thirteenth century, especially by Bonaventure.[7] In a modern study the Trinity has been presented as the highest instance of the "unity between distinct individuals" which we also experience in human life. Such a unity, far from abolishing, requires distinctions. As distinction of person makes their union possible, this does not constitute a negative limitation but a positive perfection of being. As such it may be cogently attributed to God: unity and distinction are, in God, carried to their acme.[8] My own standpoint has been grounded in the revelation of God's love in the Scriptures. It has pointed to unity-yet-distinctness as the only way to account for the paradoxes of love in God's dealings with humankind. The divine grace makes sense because God acts according to what he is: God is love, unity-yet-distinctness, One-in-Three.

Another analogy has also attracted the greatest Western theologians, especially Augustine and Thomas Aquinas.[9] They have viewed the differentiation of God's inner life on the image of the created spirit in action. It is proper to the mind to think and to will. God as mind also thinks and wills: his thinking is the Son, and his willing is the Spirit. A purely philosophical reflection could consider these as mere aspects of God. But Christian revelation implies that they are more than aspects: they are "Persons" mutually related in the process of the divine "Essence."

Another analogy has also been favored by the scholastics, especially in the Franciscan tradition.[10] God, being perfect, is perfectly fecund and self-giving. Human experience knows two sorts of fecundity: natural and spiritual. Human persons give their own substance by way of procreation and in the relationship of parents to children. Human persons also give themselves by imparting to others their love, their knowledge, their goods: spiritual relationships and friendships are born of generosity or liberality. The Three Persons may be seen in the same light: giving himself by way of nature, the Father begets the Son; by way of liberality, he breathes out the Spirit. The human modes of self-giving are thus exemplified in God. Even though we do not know the "how" of the divine Life, we can believe and adore the mystery. Clearly, this is a variation on the theme of love. Love is seen here in its dynamic fecundity, whereas the previous analogy was based on the structure of love.

None of these analogies is to be taken literally. They are analogies. This means that before being meaningful, they must be freed of whatever limits or imperfections human experience fastens to them. What remains is not a human type of fatherhood, but a relation between Giver, Given-to, and Gift. As such it may be predicated of God. This analogical purification of concepts borrowed from human experience leaves only one element applicable to God. Whatever the analogy taken as a starting point, one conclusion stands for all: the only distinctions compatible with God's utter simplicity reside in mutual relations. Father, Son, and Spirit are each the totality of the divine essence; they differ only in their reciprocal relationships. This is why the Council of Florence, as quoted above, said that in God "everything is one, except where there stands a relational opposition."[11] Already the 11th Council of Toledo in 675 insisted that Father, Son, and Spirit are relative to each other and to nothing else.[12] In the contemporary vocabulary of Simone Weil: "Trinity—relationship of God to himself."[13]

◆ ◆ ◆ ◆ ◆

A denial of the Tri-Unity of God on the ground that the classical analogies do not "prove" what they only adumbrate, could not be taken seriously. For it would misread at the start the very purpose of analogical reflection. But those who have formulated such a denial may be partially excused. The Trinitarian expressions, in their necessary abruptness, do not always convey the wealth of religious contemplation which underlies them and from which they have been born. To those who are aware of their experiential undertones, they are pregnant with the entire life of the Christian community. United to itself and to its members in love, the Church perceives in the Scripture and the tradition the shadow of God's own love expressed in human words. The God of Abraham, of Isaac, and of Jacob comes to us according to a pattern of love which is best expressed in the Trinitarian images of Scripture and in the Trinitarian analogies of the tradition. To know God as One-in-Three is to experience that God's love is not a metaphor but a reality, the ultimate reality.

Notes

1. See the excerpts from Dionysius in Elmer O'Brien, ed., *Varieties of Mystic Experience: An Anthology and Interpretation* (New York: Holt, 1964), pp. 69–78.

2. Nicholas of Cusa, *De docta ignorantia* (1444); anonymous, *The Cloud of Unknowing*, ed. McCann (Westminster, Md.: Christian Classics, 1973).

3. John of the Cross, *Coplas del alma que pena por ver a Dios*, trans. Lynda Nicholson, in Gerald Brenan, *St. John of the Cross: His Life and Poetry* (Cambridge: Cambridge University Press, 1973), p. 171.

4. There are few recent studies of the Trinity. See Mark Pontifex, *Belief in the Trinity* (London: Longmans, 1954); Karl Rahner, *The Trinity* (New York: Seabury, 1970); Raimundo Pannikar, *The Trinity and World Religions* (Madras: Christians Literature Society, 1970), also published as *The Trinity and the Religious Experience of Man* (Maryknoll, N.Y.: Orbis Books, 1973).

5. Denzinger-Schönmetzer, n. 1330.

6. Richard of St. Victor, *De Trinitate*, bk. iii, ch. 14, 18–20; see Richard of St. Victor, *La Trinité*, Sources chrétiennes, n. 63 (Paris: Le Cerf, 1959), pp. 198–201, 206–23.

7. Bonaventure, *Itinerary of the Soul into God*, ch. 6, n. 2.

8. Pontifex, *Belief in the Trinity*, pp. 67–73.

9. Austustine, *De Trinitate*, bk. x (PL 42:971–84); Thomas Aquinas, *Summa theologica*, I, q. 27, a. 3.

10. Bonaventure, *In Sententiis*, bk. I, dist. ii, art. un., q. 4.

11. See above, note 5.

12. Denzinger-Schömetzer, nn. 525–32.

13. Simone Weil, *Cahiers* II (Paris: Plon, 1953), p. 189.

PART III

Love and Willed Action

IX

Political Love

Christianity "recognizes only one kind of love, spiritual love, and does not busy itself very much in elaborating on the different ways in which this essentially common love can reveal itself. All distinctions between the many different kinds of love are essentially abolished by Christianity."[1] Kierkegaard accuses of superficiality those who are fascinated by the different forms that love can take. He may well be right. Volumes have been written to describe rival forms of love. And they have obscured the real scope and meaning of love—*agape, eros, philia*—as it emerges in the light of the Christian revelation of God, One-and-Three. But the authentic lesson of a study of love ought to be, not to persuade anyone about a theory, but to bring author and reader to the *unum necessarium*. The problem becomes, in the words of Maurice Blondel, "to know, not if this *unum necessarium* is the abstract conclusion of reasoning, but if it can itself enter as a living truth into the process of the willed action."[2] There can be no final conclusion to a study of love. For such a study shows that one has notional love on the mind, whereas real love is in the heart. There is no full stop to a reflection on love. For the reasons of the reasoning, reason must give way to the reasons of the heart. And "the heart has its reasons, which reason does not know."[3]

But what is the willed action which is called for as the authentic expression of love? Is it the act of two persons relating to each other in total oneness? Is it the self-sacrifice of the martyr who dies for his brothers and sisters? Is it the action of the militant who commits himself, out of love for the oppressed, to a revolutionary struggle? Is it the cloistered love of those who love God above all else in the mystic garden? Is it the love of God seeking the image of the Beloved in the least of the brethren?

In a sense, the way of love must be all these willed actions together. But one is asking today with more anxiety than ever before: How can I live the way of love in an unloving world? Theology has opened new avenues in trying to answer this question. Most notable is the political theology which has arisen more or less independently in several quarters. Since it must strive for the justice which is a precondition of its own development, Christian love has a political dimension. Yet Péguy's warning remains timely: "mystique" degenerates into "politique." Can one pass from the mystique of love to its political implications without dirty hands? Where does the properly Christian structure of love place love in the contemporary political horizon of theology? Is there, should there be what Arturo Paoli, in the context of Latin America, calls "political love"?[4]

◆ ◆ ◆ ◆ ◆

Political theology goes in several directions. It will be necessary to examine them briefly. I would distinguish six orientations, although this number need not be exhaustive. At any rate, the six movements that I will mention present enough distinctive features to be singled out. Three are older, and three are more recent.

A French direction is the oldest. It is concerned essentially about the politics of the gospel, the theological meaning of history, the ties between religious and civil society. Such problems have been debated in France since the heyday of Gallicanism in the seventeenth century. There is admittedly a great difference in time and mentality between Bossuet's *Politics Excerpted from the Holy Scriptures* (1677) and Jean Daniélou's *Prayer as a Political Problem* (1965). Between them there has also been the theologico-political thought of the nineteenth century, especially that of Lammenais (1782–1854).[5] Yet the general frame of reference is the same throughout. Political realities should be patterned after the demands of the religious conscience, not the other way round. As Jacques Maritain expressed it in his neo-Thomist political philosophy, there is a "primacy of the supernatural,"[6] which ought to inspire the political theory and action of the faithful. It is indeed the personal responsibility of each to choose his own stand in the political and the social order. The hierarchy cannot give guidance as to civic duties when all are equipped to perform these by their reason enlightened by their faith. Yet such social and political positions should be inspired by the vision of invisible realities which is part and parcel of the Christian outlook on the world. One can speak of the politics of the gospel. These fall specifically in the province of the laity's responsibility. If circumstances and mentalities make it inopportune to form political parties along such lines, Christians should keep their freedom to judge the very same parties in which, as citizens, they find it appropriate to struggle for a better world focused on the common good of society. This theology was particularly influential in the pastoral constitution on the Church in the Modern World, at the Second Vatican Council.

A North American direction is more pragmatic. It derives from reflection on the experience of society-building which is proper to America. It is more individualistic, being chiefly interested in the rights of the individual and in their protection from the rugged dynamics of pioneering. It is also more utopian, for it has been influenced, like North American society itself, by the utopianism of eighteenth-century philosophy and by the hopes and theories of the nineteenth-century Transcendentalists. The coloration of this theology by the American experience has made it more optimistic in its views of the political future, but less able to reflect a universal experience. In the writings of its most distinguished representative, John Courtney Murray, this theology explores the roots of Anglo-Saxon constitutional law in the demands of the human nature as reflected in the political philosophy of Aristotle and the medieval schoolmen.[7] The political insights of North America appear to be consonant with the Church's basic theological truths about man and with the contemporary requirements of pastoral solicitude. This approach had special influence in the Vatican Council's debates on religious freedom, and it is responsible for some of the central ideas of the declarations on Religious Freedom issued by the Council.

Meanwhile, some Protestant social ethicists, such as Reinhold Niebuhr, investigated the ambiguities of power which, arising even in the context of a fundamentally moral constitutional law, vitiate the best political and social systems.[8] But no extensive dialogue has taken place between the Catholic theologians of the morality of constitutional law and the Protestant theologians of the immorality of society. As a result, the original contribution of America to political theology has remained incon-

clusive and without the influence that would be propor-
tionate to its intrinsic importance.

Thirdly, an important political witness, which derives
from the accumulation of political wisdom of the
Thomist tradition, has been made by the modern popes,
especially Leo XIII, Pius XI, Pius XII, John XXIII, and
Paul VI. That many writings and speeches of Pius XII
should be seen as efforts to build a consistent political
theology I already indicated in 1959: "These documents
constitute important chapters in a possible synthesis of
Catholic thought in matters of international and national
policy today."[9] Leo XIII and Pius XI focused attention
chiefly on social questions and on the implications of
Catholic Christianity for the renovation of the social
order in view of a more equitable participation of all
citizens in the goods of this world. Due to World War II
and the post-war imbroglio and in keeping with his
personal bent, Pius XII paid special attention to the problems of the organization of peace and justice. John XXIII
and Paul VI have united social and political concerns in
encouraging Catholics to an active commitment to the
increasing socialization of modern life. What is en-
visioned by the popes as a Christian order for modern
society is a third way, between communism and
capitalism. It is neither of the left nor of the right in terms
of contemporary politics. Although Catholic moralists
have studied the thought of the popes carefully, it has
had no deep impact on the political and social forces
actually engaged in the public forum, even in traditionally Catholic nations.

There is a major reason for this lack of impact. The
political conceptions of the popes have assumed that it is
not only in accord with the gospel, but also possible and
expedient, to renounce both violence as a means of gov-

ernment and counterviolence as a means of liberation or
protest. Social relationships would then be based on
mutual trust and an equitable sharing of the goods of this
world rather than on technical superiority, racial pride,
or class struggle. This aspect of nonviolence in papal
politics is particularly noteworthy in John XXIII's encyclical *Pacem in terris,* which deserves to rank among the
great manifestos of the movement for the power of non-
violence which found its greatest spokesman in
Mahatma Gandhi.[10] The same point could be made
about Paul VI's encyclical *Populorum progressio.* Yet these
papal doctrines concerning social and political questions
have not been given the theoretical basis that they deserve. Without such a basis in Christian anthropology
they remain as valuable insights into the spontaneous
demands of the Christian conscience. But theological
elaboration ought to give them deeper grounding in the
Scriptures and in the central Christian doctrines concerning redemption and eschatology.

These three orientations in political theology have a
common point. Wishing to speak to contemporary issues, they do so on the basis of the appropriation of the
past. They carry a tradition forward. Their concern for
the past balances their interest in the present and their
hope for the future. More recently, several attempts have
been made to steer away from precedent, to break new
ground, and to create new types of political theology.

Germany, liberated from Nazism through the ruins of
World War II, faced with division between hostile political and social systems, felt the need to make the Christian faith more relevant to social and political issues than
it had traditionally been. Lutheran thought has naturally
given the tone to the social ethos of the Germanic peo-
ples. Influenced by Luther's Two-Kingdom ethics, it has
enlarged the things that are Caesar's to such a point that

the Church need not be concerned about social matters. [11] But the experience of Nazism and the struggle of the Confessing Church against the German Christians who had rallied to Hitler, showed German Protestantism that the time had arrived for taking a new look at the socio-political implications of Christianity. Catholics, treated as a foreign body by the *Kulturkampf*, associated with the ineffective Center Party of the Weimar Republic before being swamped by the political forces of the Third Reich, emerged at the same time with a new concern for their place in the body politic. Moreover, one soon felt a critical need to react against the excessive individualism of Bultmann's pietistic-existential interpretation of the New Testament and against the impasse of Bonhoeffer's religionless Christianity. Revised versions of Marxism, as in Ernst Bloch's philosophy of hope, [12] suggested also that a fruitful dialogue might be engaged between the Christian and the secular hopes for the future of man.

It is in this unique context that Johannes Metz proposed as the first task of political theology, "to be a critical correction of present-day theology inasmuch as this theology shows an extreme privatizing tendency (a tendency, that is, to center upon the private person rather than the 'public', 'political' society)." [13] The chief tool of such a critique should be eschatology, which is not private but corporate and organic. "Every eschatological theology must become a political theology, that is, a (socio-) critical theology." [14] Among Protestants, the most noted effort toward a political theology has been that of Jürgen Moltmann, whose "theology of hope" [15] also makes eschatology the critical edge of the Christian message for the world and the point from which all human achievements and institutions, including those of the Church, ought to be judged. In his more recent book, *The Crucified God* (1974), Moltmann sees eschatology and all theology in their incarnational center, the crucified Lord, thus reasserting a traditional Lutheran emphasis. This, it would seem, does not lead him to a positive view of the political future, but only to a critical scepticism before men's realizations: "Hope, which is born of the memory of the crucified Lord, leads to hope where there is nothing to hope for . . . The Christian hope, in so far as it is Christian, is the hope of those who have no future."[16] In this, Moltmann seems more realistic than Metz. But how can this theology of hope truly inspire a social commitment, which, insofar as it is social, must be a commitment to others in view of creating the structures of a better world?

The political theology of Latin America affects a much more optimistic tone. It looks directly into the future, which it attempts to reshape. It does not primarily propose a theory, but it is interested in inspiring a praxis. The dictum of Karl Marx, that "the philosophers have only *interpreted* the world, in various ways; the point, however, is to change it"[17] can be applied: "Theology, hitherto, has interpreted the world; the point, however, is to change it." Theology becomes a theology of political liberation, of world transformation. The horizon is obviously that of the Latin American republics, which, a century or so after the end of Spanish or Portuguese colonization, are still enmeshed in a neocolonialism in which a small segment of the nation, made up of professional politicians, wealthy landowners, and career soldiers, dominates and often exploits the great majority of the people. By their innate conservatism, Church institutions are a natural ally, if not an instrument, of the powers that be, so that religion truly becomes, as Marx had well perceived, an opium which helps maintain the people in subjection. In this prerevolutionary situation, a number of Latin Americans have investigated the capacity of theology to enter the social and political struggle. They have turned to social studies and social philosophies, especially Marxism, for the analytical tools they needed. Several have entered the class struggle, at least by their writings. A few, like the Colombian priest Camilo Torres, have joined the *guerilleros* in the mountains. [18] Clearly, there are serious pitfalls here. One may view this movement as a kind of apologetics which might give a Christian veneer to a purely secular-motivated revolution. But this could be a betrayal of the revolution itself and a distortion of the eschatological contents of the Christian message, too easily identified with the temporal future of humankind in a classless society. [19] In its biblical reflection, this theology takes the exodus as the paradigm of Christian behavior; but this tends to reverse the normative approach to the Scriptures by making the Old Testament primary and the New secondary. The image of the historical Jesus risks being altered in the light of great revolutionary figures like Moses or the Maccabees. [20] As a program for Christian action, liberation theology can easily lead to the consequence that Christianity, no longer an ideology of bourgeois power, becomes an ideology of revolutionary power and even a tool of revolutionary leaders or parties.

The black theology of North America is an independent variant of the same basic drive. It is born of the struggle of black Americans for their rightful place in society and the Church. At its best, black theology echoes the generous humanism of Africa, which Leopold Sedar Senghor embodied in his definition of "negritude" as "the totality of the values of the civilization of the black world" as it contributes "to the construction of the earth, to the up-building of the civilization of the Universal." [21] Yet American black theology has been little heard in Africa, except to some extent in the context

of oppression in the Republic of South Africa.[22] For it has
been more influenced by Frantz Fanon's resentful meditations on violence[23] than by Senghor's serene, yet more
effective, reflections on civilization. In its extreme form it
has fallen into particularism, assuming that God is better
represented by the specific features by which black people and black culture differ from other people and other
cultures.

◆ ◆ ◆ ◆ ◆

What is the place of Christian love in political theology?
The only author who, to my knowledge, discusses the
matter at length, is Arturo Paoli. "Political love," as Paoli
describes it,

> is the complement and the richness of the love of friend-
> ship because only this reaching out toward the world in a
> responsible and involved way enriches friendship by giv-
> ing it value and dynamism. And it is friendship which
> makes possible this dedication of oneself to the world. We
> cannot think of political love outside of a community and a
> community cannot be thought of outside this political
> love. The whole Gospel invites the disciple to take a posi-
> tion of watchfulness and concrete search in the historical
> situations in which the values of freedom, charity, and
> hope are to be incarnated, it invites him to become in-
> volved concretely and dangerously in history.[24]

In other words, political love is the broader dimension of
friendship. It is friendship urging us to enter the political
arena on behalf of the poor and the oppressed. Political
love thus posits a major question in the context of liberation from oppression: Can Christian love lead to systematic violence? Can it lead to the counterviolence of
the oppressed against the institutional violence of an
oppressive status quo? Does the structure of Christian
love allow this love to make use of violence to reach its
purposes?

The political theology of Germany gives an ambiguous answer. "Love," for Johannes Metz, "postulates a determined criticism of pure power." That is, love condemns situations where human relationships are dominated by naked power. Yet "there may be circumstances where love itself could demand actions of a *revolutionary character*."[25] I take it that in such a situation the power of the revolution would not be naked power: it would be controlled power at the service of justice.

The Latin American political theology, impressed among other things by the example of Camilo Torres and the aura that his death as a *guerillero* has given him, goes much further. Paoli sees Che Guevara and Camilo Torres as effectively "desiring and working for freedom," the ultimate type of which is Jesus Christ, though they are not, "completely and definitively, saviors or liberators."[26] The Brazilian Protestant, Rubem Alves, envisions a dialectic which is not without connection with Luther's conception of man as sinner and saint:

> Liberation . . . is the sole determination of the God who is the Suffering Slave. But in order to liberate the oppressed, the lamb must become a lion, the slave must become a warrior . . . There is violence in the process. God does not wait for the dragon to become a lamb . . . The power of God destroys what makes the world unfree. This use of power looks like violence . . . But . . . what looks like the violence of the lion is really the power of counterviolence, that is, power used against those who generate, support, and defend the violence of a world of masters and slaves . . . Violence is power aimed at paralysis. Counterviolence is aimed at making man free for experimentation. The use of violence is in the politics of the Messiah an instrument to liberate even the master against whom it is used.[27]

Applying to this dialectic the categories of Luther's theology, Alves continues: "This is the dark side of the politics of liberation: the 'No,' love as power against, wrath against, the oppressors, the *opus alienum Dei* . . . But the *opus alienum Dei* is done for the sake of the *opus proprium Dei,* the No is for the sake of the Yes, the destruction for the sake of the building up, the liberation from the past for the sake of the liberation for the future."[28]

From the point of view of the Scriptures, it is obviously an abuse to equate counterviolence with God's own works, with the politics of the Messiah and with the *opus alienum Dei.* On the one hand, no man has a right to take upon himself the *opus alienum Dei.* On the other, this dialectic rests upon an anthropomorphic concept of God that may be found in parts of the Pentateuch, but is not that of the prophets or of the New Testament. Moreover, it is politically naive to imagine that counterviolence is always right and holy. History is filled with unjustified revolutions and with revolutions that have betrayed the people. One may even wonder if violence is not structurally unable, by virtue of its own impetus, to establish an order of justice and peace. One may also ask who in a society marked by oppression is free enough to establish an order of freedom and love. Simone Weil, who was by no means a partisan of the social *status quo,* rightly noted: "Never yet in history has a regime of slavery fallen under the blows of slaves."[29]

Indeed, the immeasurable misery caused by the great revolutions of Western history, such as the French Revolution of 1789 or the Soviet Revolution of 1917, would tend to support, by contrast, James Douglass's theology of nonviolence: "To love is to suffer in joy, for the perfect union sought by love can be approached only through sacrifice. Love's price of suffering extended across the world is the price of redeeming man's violence . . . Love is the Power, but a Power incarnate on the cross."[30]

The political theology of recent times has done little to throw light on the central problem of social ethics: How can I follow the way of love if my educational matrix has made me a member or an ally of an oppressive social system? How can I follow the way of love if on the contrary my environment has made me an agent or a fellow-traveler of the struggle of the oppressed for liberation?

This is not asking if there may be a Christian of the left and a Christian of the right. But it is asking if the same structure of Christian love can allow the faithful to be indifferently on the political left or the political right. The political theologies of Latin America assume or conclude that Christians must be of the left. But the case for this position seems to be based on political and social theories rather than on the structure of Christian love. The political theology of Germany stands aloof of clear political involvement, although it sees liberation movements as expressing the human hope of our day. The political theology of the popes, which takes the power of non-violence as the heart of a Christian strategy for justice and peace, remains uncommitted to the contemporary struggles which, since the passing of Gandhi, are all engaged in some form of violence.

I will now attempt to show in what direction the structure of love, as I have analyzed it, seems to point. The problem hangs on the relationship between love and justice.

The present investigation has identified justice as a precondition for Christian *agape*. Justice is the process by which we make ourselves neighbors to others so that these may respond with love. The selective love of friendship presupposes a basis of universal love, which itself rests on the justice which is extended to us. Love and justice therefore form a three-tier system of human relationships. If justice leads to universal love, within whose horizon selective love flourishes, it follows that the primary virtue of a Christian society is the organization of the justice without which love cannot fully grow. But this raises critical questions concerning the general history of humankind and the present state of the world. The establishment of an order of justice in society has so far in history been a near impossibility, which has inspired intriguing utopias but no effective political system. And, despite the increasingly close economic and cultural ties among nations, the present world is far from a universal order of justice. In these conditions, is Christian love also a utopia? Granted the occasional exception of great saints, should not the faithful rest satisfied with what they can do to survive injustice, and be resigned to live with a universal love which falls short of universality and with a selective love which remains stunted because society does not provide it with a suitable environment?

The context of Christian love is the worldwide Church and, wider still, the world itself. The attempt to live perfectly the several levels of love—the compassion that creates justice, *agape*, friendship—often flounders in the inescapable tension between three elements: the fundamental need to love and to be loved, the sublimation of this need into mystical union with God in the community of discipleship, and the impact of the cosmic and social forces which, opposing the temporal interests of various men, bring humankind into a spiralling escalation of conflict, hatred, and violence. The Christian life does not unfold within the closed walls of a mystic garth. It takes place in the midst of the world. Whether this is better symbolized by the bustling marketplace of older societies or by the stock exchange of newer societies, the problem is the same: How to follow the way of love where justice does not reign?

This is not only a Christian dilemma. The Bhagavad
Gita poses the problem in the context of Hinduism: soldiers must fight the enemy, Arjuna is told by Krishna,
yet without hatred.[31] The followers of all peaceful religious prophets meet the problem as soon as they experience the contrast between believing community and un-
believing world. In the Johannine writings of the New
Testament, the disciples live in the light and according to
the light, yet in a world of darkness. Indeed, "the light
shines in the darkness, a darkness that did not overcome
it" (John 1:5). Yet even the saints confess that at times
darkness nearly overcomes the light in their life. And
there are periods in church history when the collective
darkness of the world overshadows the dimming light of
Christian love.

In its struggle for survival in the dark night of some
centuries, the Church attempted to institutionalize
Christian love in order to protect it. As the faith had been
stabilized in creeds, so there were endeavors to secure
the proper institutional framework for a life of love. If
love could be socially embodied in regular patterns of
behavior, acquired habit would counteract the social
forces which foster unlove by institutionalizing injustice.
But while the Church until recent times was relatively
successful in regulating marital love, it met with notori-
ous failure in the broader area of politics and social relationships. In 1139 the Second Council of the Lateran
vainly tried to stem two major trends that have been at
the source of the corporate injustices of modern society:
the acquisition of power through the manipulation of
money, and the drive to domination through coercion.

In the first area of concern the Council used the
strongest possible language to condemn usury, a condemnation which was repeated throughout the Middle
Ages: "We condemn the insatiable rapacity of usurers,

which is detestable, opposed to divine and human laws, banned by Scripture in the Old and the New Testament."[32] Usurers will be refused the sacraments and Christian burial. In the second area of concern, the Council tried to impose a weekly truce on all warring parties, from Wednesday evening to Monday morning,[33] and two yearly truces, from the first Sunday in Advent to the octave of the Epiphany, and from Quinquagesima Sunday to the octave of Easter.[34] And it forbade using against Christians the instruments of war that could then kill men at a distance, namely the ballista and the crossbow. Such inventions the Council called "death-provoking and hateful to God."[35]

Had these warnings been heeded, the growth of the capitalist system out of the commercial life of the later Middle Ages might have been less oppressive for the poor.[36] And the instruments of overkill that our age has devised would have remained in the realm of science fiction. But however pleasant it may be to dream about what might have been, our social context is marked by systematic injustice, by institutional violence, by the desperate violence of terrorism. It is in this world that Christians have to find the way of love. And such a world has itself so influenced the Christian mentality that the Church's timid interventions in the area of social justice and of peace are often resented by Christians themselves. The social encyclicals of the contemporary popes have had little impact on Catholic thought and practice. They assume that a third way is realistically possible between the violence of predominant institutions and the violence of the revolution. They have therefore been dismissed as irrelevant by the manipulators of the market, and as tools of capitalism by social revolutionaries. Yet it seems to be a law of macrosocial dynamics that the extremes make the stronger impact in the short run, whereas in the long run it is the mediating force that ensures the possibility of organic renovation. As to the Church's interventions in the face of war, they have been largely restricted to moral condemnations of violence. The few practical measures that were taken—as when Pius XII assisted Jews persecuted by the Nazis or when Paul VI sent food to Biafra—were widely misunderstood, being seen as insufficient by some and as instruments of war by others. The Church of South America is commonly accused of favoring the status quo by the weight of its own inertia. Yet the positions of the Latin American bishops at the conference of Medellín look forward to drastic changes in social structures destined to make society less oppressive.[37] In all these instances, the difficulty appears when one tries to apply theoretical views to the human reality which constitutes society. Is it possible to transform the structures of oppressive society without crushing anyone in the process?

Political love is universal love which, seeking to enable others to respond and anticipating its own response to others, strives for the universal order of justice. Such a love is not violent, for it has patience, kindness, forbearance, trust, hope, power to endure—the qualities that St. Paul associates with love in 1 Cor. 13. In the rare situations where violence is inescapable, the person who practices universal love mitigates the course of violence by raising the hope, be it against all odds, of becoming lovable to those who are, for the moment, his enemies. Those who have the responsibility for promoting justice are precisely the Christians in search of the Kingdom. For justice is a precondition of love.

This is the basic lesson of the present study in the area of political love. But two additional points must be emphasized regarding the dilemma of loving in an unloving world.

Oneness with another person in selective love constitutes the heart of the Christian structure of love. Total
identification with humankind appears then as the eschatological limit of love. The symbols of the Kingdom in
the parables of the New Testament point to the end as
the manifestation of God as all in all and to the *parousia* as
unveiling the depths of human relationships. This is the
end, because it is the ultimate purpose of history. There
is nothing for humanity to seek beyond the full discovery
of the mystery of humankind, which is obtained in the
union of all in God. In the period that still separates us
from eschatological fulfillment, Christian love should
inspire an anthropology that meets the requirements of
the Christian revelation as well as the needs of the times.
I have outlined such an anthropology in the last chapters
of *Woman in Christian Tradition*. [38] What I perceive to be
the true scope of the political theologies and the
theologies of liberation of recent times is that they stress
the corporate, organic, collective aspects of man, who
becomes a person only in interrelationship with others.
The individualism that grew out of the Renaissance is
doomed. The struggle for liberation, the desire to change
the structures of society, the call for worldwide justice,
may not be the final stages before the Kingdom. Yet they
at least witness to the human desire for fulfillment in
total oneness. At their best, they prepare the Kingdom.
But the final revolution cannot be made by those who
rise in anger. It will be made by those who, in giving
themselves totally to others, show that they are able to
sacrifice themselves for humankind. In fusing several I's
into a We, love makes it possible to experience mankind
as We. Without such an experience political love remains
a theory. With such an experience it can become a praxis.

There is still another lesson to learn, the deepest yet
also the hardest. The structure of love is not autarkic.

It shows human persons hungering for self-transcendence. But self-transcendence is a contradiction in terms, unless we can be raised above ourselves by one who is greater than we. The Marxist or neo-Marxist conception of self-transcendence as the indefinite future of man[39] is only a sweet delusion. It is the opium which, in Communist countries, helps the generations of today accept being sacrificed to those of tomorrow. But there is no warrant in history, in science, in philosophy, for the assumption that the generations of tomorrow will be any happier than those of yesterday. Faith itself guarantees no such thing. It is affirmed by Marxism, precisely at the point where Marxism is most vulnerable.[40]

As embodied in the dying and the rising of Christ, the Christian structure of love teaches that the way to victory is self-denial in defeat. And the deeper the self-denial, the greater the possibility of ultimate victory. This is not a political program and one cannot speak of the "politics of God." One can speak, however, of the overcoming of politics by the God who raised from the dead One who refused to join the political struggle of the Zealots because his love was wider than theirs, and yet who was falsely condemned as a Zealot.[41] True Christian love is not political, but transpolitical. That is, whatever the political commitments one has chosen in keeping with reasonable hopes for the betterment of humankind through socio-political structures, Christian love realizes that all political projects nurture in themselves what Simone Weil, following Plato, called "the beast," "the social idol."[42] They always contain the seeds of new oppressions. Love will always have to reach toward others in spite of the institutions of society. Mankind is saved in spite of itself.

The love that is in God, the model of all human love, reminds us that, however important is justice on earth, the ultimate purpose of life is not to establish permanent structures of justice and peace in the world. It is to prepare ourselves for the vision of God and for total participation in the divine life. To Pilate, who represented an oppressive power, Jesus answered: "My kingdom does not belong to this world" (John 18:36). The Kingdom is not ahead of us in humanity's future. It is IN GOD.

Notes

1. Sören Kierkegaard, *Works of Love* (London: Collins, 1962), p. 144.

2. Maurice Blondel, *L'Action* (1893) (Paris: Presses Universitaires, 1950), p. 340.

3. Pascal, *Pensées*, n. 477; Jacques Chevalier, ed., *Pascal, Oeuvres Complètes* (Paris: Gallimard, 1964), p. 1221.

4. Arturo Paoli, *The Freedom to Be Free* (Maryknoll, N.Y.: Orbis Books, 1973), p. 89.

5. During and after the French Revolution a very thorough political theology was elaborated in royalist and ultramontane directions. See Louis de Bonald, *Théorie du pouvoir politique et religieux dans la société civile* (1796); Joseph de Maistre, *Du Pape* (1819). Lammenais adapted these views to a democratic, yet ultramontane, conception: *De la religion considérée dans ses rapports avec l'ordre politique et civil* (1825–1826).

6. This is the original title of Maritain's book translated as *The Things That Are Not Caesar's* (New York: Scribner's, 1931; Plainview, N.Y.: Books for Libraries, 1972). See his *Scholasticism and Politics* (London: Macmillan, 1940); *Man and the State* (Chicago: University of Chicago Press, 1956); Jean Daniélou, *The Lord of History: Reflections on the Inner Meaning of History*, trans. Nigel Abercrombie (London: Longmans, and Chicago: Regnery, 1958); Daniélou, *Prayer as a Political Problem*, trans. J.W. Kirwan (New York: Sheed & Ward, 1967); Jean-Marie Paupert, *Politics of the Gospel*, trans. Roy Gregor (New York: Holt, 1969).

7. John Courtney Murray, *We Hold These Truths* (New York: Sheed & Ward, 1960); *The Problem of Religious Freedom* (Westminster, Md.: Newman, 1965). See Eric Voegelin, *The New Science of Politics*

(Chicago: University of Chicago Press, 1952); *Order and History*, 3 vols. (Baton Rouge: Louisiana State University Press, 1956–1957); George Grant, *Technology and Empire: Perspectives on North America* (Toronto: House of Anansi Press, 1969); George Tavard, *Catholicism, USA* (New York: Paulist, 1969).

8. Reinhold Niebuhr, *Moral Man and Immoral Society* (New York: Scribner, 1960).

9. Tavard, *The Church, the Layman and the Modern World* (New York: Macmillan, 1959), p. 48. One should recognize that the popes of the earlier nineteenth century, especially Gregory XVI and Pius IX, followed another kind of political theology, tied to the concept of royal legitimacy. The action of Leo XIII in updating the papal political theology was drastic and quite remarkable.

10. See James Douglass, *The Non-Violent Cross: A Theology of Revolution and Peace* (New York: Macmillan, 1969).

11. See George W. Forrell, *Faith Active in Love: An Investigation of the Principles Underlying Luther's Social Ethics* (Minneapolis: Augsburg, 1964).

12. Ernst Bloch, *Das Prinzip Hoffnung*, 3 vols. (Frankfurt: Suhrkamp Verlag, 1969); *A Philosophy of the Future* (New York: Seabury, 1970).

13. Johannes Metz, *Theology of the World* (New York: Seabury, 1969), p. 107.

14. *Ibid.*, p. 115.

15. Jürgen Moltmann, *The Theology of Hope* (New York: Harper and Row, 1967).

16. Jürgen Moltmann, *Man: Christian Anthropology in the Conflicts of the Present*, trans. John Sturdy (Philadelphia: Fortress, 1974), p. 117.

17. "Thesis on Feuerbach," Thesis XI, in Karl Marx and Friedrich Engels, *On Religion* (Moscow: Foreign Language Publishing House, 1957), p. 72.

18. See Germán Guzmán Campos, *El Padre Camilo Torres* (Mexico: Siglo Veintiuno, 1968); Camilo Torres, *Revolutionary Writings* (New York: Harper and Row, 1972). To forestall criticism, I may mention that in order to appreciate the Latin American political theology better, I personally visited Colombia in 1973. I was already acquainted with pre-Allende Chile.

19. This is particularly clear in the "humanistic messianism" of Rubem Alves (*A Theology of Human Hope* [St. Meinrad, Ind.: Abbey Press, 1972], p. 141). The belief that one can change man by changing institutions is of course a dangerous illusion. Gustavo Gutiérrez gives the impression of expecting a "new man" to appear in the future (*Teología de la Liberación* [Lima: CEP, 1971], and *A Theology of Liberation:*

History, Politics, and Salvation, trans. Sister Caridad Inda and John Eagleson [Maryknoll; N.Y.: Orbis Books, 1973], pp. 189, 213, ff.). This is a new form of the old expectation of a millenium. The ties between liberation and Christian utopianism are clear in some of the recent American writings, such as Frederick Herzog, ed., *The Theology of the Liberating Word* (New York: Abingdon, 1970); *Liberation Theology* (New York: Seabury, 1972); Rosemary Ruether, *Liberation Theology* (New York: Paulist-Newman, 1973). These writings are more related to the German and the Latin American political theology than to the previous political theology of North America.

20. Rafael Avida, *Teología, Evangelización y Liberación* (Bogotá: Ediciones Paulinas, 1973), pp. 80–83.

21. Leopold Sedar Senghor, "Pierre Teilhard de Chardin et la politique africaine," *Cahiers Pierre Teilhard de Chardin,* III (1962) 20 and 16.

22. Mokgethi Motlabi, ed., *Essays on Black Theology* (Johannesburg; University Christian Movement, 1971). This book was "banned" shortly after publication, by the authorities of the Republic of South Africa. On American black theology, see Albert Cleage, *The Black Messiah* (New York: Sheed & Ward, 1968); James Cone, *Black Theology and Black Power* (New York: Seabury, 1969) and *Black Theology of Liberation* (Philadelphia: Lippincott, 1970).

23. Frantz Fanon, *The Wretched of the Earth,* trans. Constance Farrington (New York: Grove, 1965).

24. Paoli, *The Freedom To Be Free,* p. 88. Paoli's analysis of love divides it into four categories, love in the man-woman relationship, friendship, political love, and virginal love (virginity for the Kingdom).

25. Metz, *Theology of the World,* pp. 119–20.

26. Paoli, *The Freedom To Be Free,* p. 88.

27. Alves, *A Theology of Human Hope,* p. 125.

28. *Ibid.,* pp. 126–27.

29. Simone Weil, *Oppression and Liberty,* trans. Arthur Wills and John Petrie (Amherst: University of Massachusetts Press, 1973), p. 117.

30. Douglass, *The Non-Violent Cross,* p. 290.

31. Juan Mascaro, tr., *The Bhagavad Gita* (Baltimore: Penguin, 1962), pp. 48–55.

32. *Conciliorum Oecumenicorum Decreta* (Basle: Herder, 1962), p. 176, n. 13.

33. *Ibid.,* pp. 175–76, n. 12.

34. *Ibid.*, p. 176, n. 14.

35. *Ibid.*, p. 179, n. 29.

36. Canon 1543, in the code of Canon Law, still embodies the anti-usury principle, but with concessions which make it compatible with the placing of money at a risk. It is the risk that is seen as justifying profit.

37. Second General Conference of the Episcopate of Latin America, Medellín, Colombia, August 20 to September 6, 1968. Full text of the report in *Criterio* (Buenos Aires), Oct. 24, 1968, pp. 756–804, and also in *The Church in the Present-Day Transformation of Latin America in the Light of the Council,* ed. Louis Colonnese (Washington: Latin America Bureau, United States Catholic Conference, 1970). Vol. II, Conclusions. The second chapter, on peace, is particularly relevant for the situation of political theology in Latin America. See Segundo Galilea, ed., *La Vertiente Política de la Pastoral* (Quito: Instituto Pastoral Latino Americano, 1970); Camilo Moncada, ed., *Liberación en America Latina* (Bogotá: Editorial America Latina, 1971).

38. Tavard, *Woman in Christian Tradition* (Notre Dame, Ind.: University of Notre Dame Press, 1973), pp. 187–229.

39. See the writings of Roger Garaudy, especially *From Anathema to Dialogue: A Marxist Challenge to the Christian Churches,* trans. Luke O'Neill (New York: Herder, 1966); *Marxisme du XXe siècle* (Paris: Collection 10/18, 1966). Similar trends are clear in Ernst Bloch, *Philosophy of the Future,* and in the poetry of Communist poets, such as Pablo Neruda in Chile or Aragon in France.

40. See Simone Weil, "On the Contradictions of Marxism," in *Oppression and Liberty,* pp. 147–155.

41. See Gerard S. Sloyan, *Jesus on Trial: The Development of the Passion Narratives and Their Historical and Ecumenical Implications* (Philadelphia: Fortress, 1973), pp. 119, 128–29.

42. Simone Weil, *Cahiers* III (Paris: Plon, 1956), p. 246; *Oppression and Liberty,* p. 165.

Bibliographical Note

PSYCHOLOGICAL

Fromme, Erich, *The Art of Loving.* New York: Harper and Row, 1965.

May, Rollo, *Love and Will.* New York: Norton, 1969.

PSYCHO-ANALYTICAL

Reik, Theodor. *Of Love and Lust.* New York: Grove, 1957.

Sorokin, Pitirim. *The Ways and Power of Love.* Boston: Beacon, 1964.

PHILOSOPHICAL

D'Arcy, Martin. *The Mind and Heart of Love.* New York: Holt, 1947.

Johann, Robert. *The Meaning of Love.* New York: Paulist-Newman, 1966.

SOCIOLOGICAL

Toner, Jules. *The Experience of Love.* Washington: Corpus, 1968.

PHENOMENOLOGICAL

Sadler, William. *Existence and Love: A New Approach in Existential Phenomenology.* New York: Scribner's, 1970.

LITERARY

De Rougement, Denis. *L'Amour et l'occident; Love in the Western World.* Translated by Montgomery Belgion. New York: Pantheon, 1956.

———. *Les Mythes de l'amour*. Paris: Gallimard, 1961.

Ortega y Gasset, Jose. *Estudios sobre el Amor; On Love*. Translated by Toby Talbot. New York: Meridian, 1958.

THEOLOGICAL

Harper, Ralph. *Human Love, Existential and Mystical*. Baltimore: Johns Hopkins, 1966.

McIntyre, John. *On the Love of God*. New York: Harper, 1962.

Nygren, Anders. *Agapè and Eros*. Philadelphia: Westminster, 1969.

William, Daniel Day. *The Spirit and the Forms of Love*. New York: Harper and Row, 1968.

For biblical works, see notes following the chapters. For a general approach from the point of view of "friendship," see Pedro Laín Entralgo, *Sobre la Amistad* (Madrid: Revista de Occidente, 1972).